W9-CDF-008

By Joe McGinniss

The Miracle of Castel di Sangro

The Last Brother

Cruel Doubt

Blind Faith

Fatal Vision

Going to Extremes

Heroes

The Dream Team

The Selling of the President 1968

HAROLD ROTH / HORSEPHOTOS

The Big Horse

Joe McGinniss

Simon & Schuster

NEW YORK • LONDON • TORONTO • SYDNEY

SIMON & SCHUSTER
Rockefeller Center
1230 Avenue of the Americas
New York, NY 10020

Copyright © 2004 by Joe McGinniss
All rights reserved,
including the right of reproduction
in whole or in part in any form.

SIMON & SCHUSTER and colophon are registered trademarks
of Simon & Schuster, Inc.

For information about special discounts for bulk purchases,
please contact Simon & Schuster Special Sales at
1-800-456-6798 or business@simonandschuster.com

Designed by Paul Dippolito

Manufactured in the United States of America

10 9 8 7 6 5 4 3 2 1

Library of Congress Cataloging-in-Publication Data is available.

ISBN 0-7432-6079-1

Acknowledgments

I would like to thank the following people, who helped to make my time at Saratoga in 2003 so educational and enjoyable: Pierre Bellocq, Pierre Bellocq, Jr., Remi Bellocq, Cot and Anne Campbell, Ocala and Debbie Cedano, Sean Clancy, Rodrigo Duran, Tom Gilcoyne, Charlie Hayward, John Hertler, Joe Hirsch, Allen Jerkens, Don Little, Jr., Terry Meyocks, Richard Migliore, Anne Palamountain, Todd Pletcher, Jose Santos, Mrs. Whitney (Lucy Lyle) Tower, and Jean-Luc Samyn—who would have, I'm sure, if he hadn't broken his leg.

I would also like to thank David Rosenthal and (not for the first time) Michael Korda at Simon & Schuster, whose enthusiasm made this book possible. I'd like to thank my lawyer, agent, and friend, Dennis Holahan, for showing he has a heart as well as a mind.

I am, of course, enormously indebted to Philip George Johnson and his family: Mary Kay, Kathy, Karen, Emma, and sons-in-law Don Brockway and Noel Michaels. P. G. Johnson taught me a lot about racing, but more about life, at a time when I thought I was too old to learn.

And I would especially like to thank my children, Christine Marque, Suzanne Boyer, Joe McGinniss, Jr., Matthew McGinniss, and James McGinniss, for their love, confidence, and encouragement during some difficult years.

For Anne

1 Saratoga

P.G. with Volponi

SKIP DICKSTEIN

1 It was raining and still dark when I got to the barn.

The barn was located behind the Oklahoma training track at Saratoga Race Course.

Saratoga is in upstate New York. The training track had been named in the early years, when people had to walk rather than drive to reach it, and its distance from the main track made it seem as remote as Oklahoma.

I squished through the mud, amid dark silhouettes of horses. It was 6 A.M. on the Monday of the last week of July 2003—the first week of Saratoga's six-week racing season. It also was the first time in more than thirty years that I'd been in the Saratoga stable area.

"Can I help you?"

"I'm looking for Mr. Johnson."

"What the hell for?"

The voice was like sandpaper. The speaker was a short man with rounded shoulders. He was wearing a rain jacket and baseball cap, and standing, stooped, beneath a wooden overhang in front of a stall about halfway down the shed row. I hadn't seen him since 1971, and I hadn't actually met him even then, but I knew this had to be P.G.

– 3 –

"I called you last night," I said. "You told me I could meet you here this morning."

"Why would I have said that? Oh, Christ, you must be the guy I'm supposed to be nice to so my daughter doesn't lose her goddamned job."

I could hardly see him in the dark, through the rain.

"If you have any questions," he said, "I'll try to answer them. If it's not inconvenient, I might even tell you the truth. But I hope you don't have too many. Ocala's my assistant, but don't bother him, he's a son of a bitch. And try to stay out of the way. I'm a working horse trainer, not a goddamned tourist destination."

He turned, and started to shuffle back toward the end of the barn, to the small, dirt-floored cubicle that served as his office at Saratoga.

"I wanted to meet you thirty-two years ago," I called after him.

"You're late."

"The first time I ever bet a hundred dollars was on a horse of yours. 1970. It was the day of the Travers. Cote-de-Boeuf. Jean Cruguet rode him. Four to one in the morning line. He finished out of the money."

"You shouldn't bet. I quit that foolishness years ago."

"Later on, can I see Volponi?"

"Yeah, but for Christ's sake don't try to pet him, unless you want to start typing with your toes."

2 I was born in New York City in 1942, the year P. G. Johnson bought his first horse. My father's father, an MIT graduate, had been an architect in Boston. My mother's father, an Irish immigrant, had been a New York City fireman. Given such a disparity in bloodlines, if they'd been Thoroughbred horses, my parents would not have been bred to each other. As it was, the results were problematic.

We lived in an apartment in Forest Hills, Queens. My father—who had lost both his parents in the influenza epidemic of 1918, when he was two—was not a physically active man, but he did enjoy listening to sporting events on the radio.

I remember Red Barber describing Cookie Lavagetto's two-outs-in-the-ninth pinch-hit double off the Ebbets Field right-field wall that not only gave the Brooklyn Dodgers a stunning 3-2 victory, but deprived Yankees pitcher Bill Bevens of the first no-hitter in World Series history. That was in 1947, when I was four.

I also remember my father and I listening to Clem McCarthy's call of the 1948 Kentucky Derby, won by Citation, Eddie Arcaro aboard, with Calumet stablemate Coaltown finishing second.

My father—who had attended MIT, but had not graduated—did well enough in his business of preparing blueprints for New York City architects to enable us to move to a new home in Rye, in Westchester County.

There, on black-and-white TV, I not only saw Bobby Thompson's home run in 1951, but I watched Dark Star beat Native Dancer in the 1953 Kentucky Derby. I also remember seeing Nashua beat Swaps in the 1955 match race at Chicago's Washington Park (the biggest, it was said, since Seabiscuit vs. War Admiral), and being aghast when Willie Shoemaker misjudged the finish line aboard Gallant Man and lost the 1957 Kentucky Derby. Tom Fool, Bold Ruler, Round Table, Sword Dancer: These were heroes of my childhood sporting universe on a par with Joe DiMaggio, Ted Williams, and Jackie Robinson.

Eventually, my father took me to baseball games at Yankee Stadium and the Polo Grounds, and to Fordham University football games, but never to the races. My mother explained that no matter how splendid the Kentucky Derby might have seemed on television, the racetrack was a sordid place, populated by men even more disreputable than those who frequented taverns, or, to use her term, "gin mills." I was to follow my father's example and give both places a wide berth when I grew older. In response, I developed an extravagant fantasy life, in which I lived in a gin mill next to a racetrack, dividing my time equally between them.

That my father might have had more personal knowledge of either barrooms or racetracks than he let on was not something that occurred to me until one day—I must have been about ten at the time—when I spotted, among the many thick tomes on architectural history and design theory that filled the bookshelves of his study, a slim volume titled *Win, Place and Show.*

I took it down and began to read it, paying special attention to the portions my father had already underlined. It was not a long book, nor was it unduly complex, and I soon came to understand that the attainment of almost limitless wealth was well within the grasp of any horseplayer who learned to apply the author's handicapping and wagering principles.

My mother found me before I could finish it. She grabbed the book from my hands as if it was an illustrated edition of *Peyton Place.*

"Where did you get that?"

I pointed to my father's study.

"Well, I'll be speaking to him about *that!*" She walked off with the book under her arm and I never saw it again. Nor did my father and I ever discuss the incident. There was a lot that we never discussed.

As a result, the racetrack—any racetrack—came to seem the most alluring destination on earth. I vowed to visit one on my own, as soon as I was old enough to take the train into New York City and to ride the New York subway by myself.

This happened when I was twelve. I went to Jamaica Race Track, in the borough of Queens. You were supposed to be twenty-one to bet, but I was tall for my age.

Jamaica closed in the late fifties, but by 1959, as a senior in high school, I was cutting afternoon classes in order to go to the new Aqueduct, farther out in Queens, near JFK Airport, which was named Idlewild at the time.

I made my first trip to Saratoga in August 1962, for the Travers Stakes. Jaipur beat Ridan by a nose. A lot of people don't realize that Jaipur never won another race—which is neither here nor there, but it's the sort of useless thing you remember from having spent a lot of time around the track.

For a while—stuck in college in central Massachusetts— I became a regular at such sorry venues as Suffolk Downs in Boston and Lincoln Downs and Narragansett in Rhode Island. I lost money on horses that were, on their best day, Thoroughbreds in name only, and I didn't see many on their best day.

During vacations, I moved up in class. I got to Hialeah in the winter, Garden State and Pimlico in the spring, and Saratoga and Monmouth in the summer. By the time I graduated—which was a closer call than it should have been, in large part because I'd spent more time with the *Morning*

Telegraph and *Daily Racing Form* than with my textbooks—I'd probably been to every Thoroughbred horse-racing track north of the Mason-Dixon Line and east of the Mississippi, and to quite a few that lay beyond.

In 1963, I hitchhiked to Louisville for the Kentucky Derby, snuck in through the stable entrance before dawn, and with my last two dollars made the most wonderful bet of my life—on Chateaugay.

Ridden by the magisterial Panamanian Braulio Baeza, Chateaugay beat the three favorites—Candy Spots, No Robbery, and Never Bend—and paid $20.80 to win.

In those days, there were two races on the Churchill Downs card after the Derby. I parlayed my Chateaugay profit and won them both. That night, I booked a suite at the Brown Hotel, which was as fancy as you could get in Louisville in the early sixties, and entertained a lovely secretary from Fort Wayne. The next day, instead of hitchhiking back to Massachusetts, I flew first-class on Allegheny.

But after that, my life at the track was mostly downhill. Once out of college, I broadened my range to include not only Chicago's Arlington Park, but even Hollywood Park and Santa Anita in California. All too often, however, and with excuses that grew flimsier over time, I found myself at such forlorn locales as Pocono Downs, Yakima Meadows, and Ak-Sar-Ben (and what else could they do with a racetrack in

Omaha except name it for Nebraska spelled backward?). I went to the track wherever I was, and where I was was too often the result of there being a track in the vicinity. In December 1967—a month before the Tet Offensive—I even went to the races in Saigon.

———

Through it all, Saratoga remained a beacon. It was the promised land: Camelot, or Xanadu, where the breezes were fresh, the horses fast, and the women beautiful. And where one's bankroll would magically replenish itself overnight.

I think it is safe to say that Saratoga has been written about more than all other American racetracks combined, and almost always in a reverential tone. Through the 1950s and 1960s, I read a lot of that writing and it did much to shape my perception of the place, even if my clearest memory of the 1962 Travers was of how crowded it had been, and how nearly impossible it was to see the race.

I knew Red Smith's famous directions for reaching Saratoga from New York City: Take the Thruway north for 175 miles, get off at Exit 14, turn west on Union Avenue, and go back a hundred years in time. And I believed, with his *Herald-Tribune* compatriot, Joe Palmer, that "a man who would change it would stir champagne."

Saratoga had been bathed in a special aura from the start. Already famed for having hosted one of the more significant battles of the Revolutionary War, as well as for its underground springs, which were said to have myriad medicinal properties, the town had developed into a posh summer resort (popular among "artificial aristocrats," a local newspaper said) even before Thoroughbred horses began to race there, in August 1863.

At first, the racing served only as a minor diversion for high-stakes gamblers—a way to pass the time between hangover and cocktail hour—and most of the press attention it attracted was negative.

"Men shout and grow frantic in their frenzy as the horses whirl round the track," the *New York Tribune* wrote in 1865, "and as they close upon the goal the spasm becomes stifling, ecstatic and bewildering."

As if that was a bad thing.

From the start, Saratoga was known for its short season (for decades, only four weeks in August), for the high quality of its horses, and for the inordinately high percentage of spectators with names such as Vanderbilt, Whitney, and Phipps.

Their presence—in many cases, the high-quality horses belonged to them—and their willingness to spend the money necessary to keep their private playground impervious to change were what provided Saratoga, for years, with its special ambience.

There were other notable racetracks in America—and by the start of the 1970s, I probably had been to them all, except Keeneland in Lexington, Kentucky—but for a concentrated commingling of old money and new horses in a pastoral setting, Saratoga was unmatched.

More than a hundred years earlier, the *New York Times* had described the scene as consisting of "pure air, fresh breezes . . . [and] a great deal of very weak human nature." Those still seemed the perfect ingredients for a summer vacation, especially with good horses to spice the blend. In 1971, having finished a novel set at Hialeah, I tried to arrange such an interlude for myself, signing a contract with Alfred A. Knopf Inc. to write a book about that season's racing at Saratoga.

At the start of August, I moved into a rented house on the outskirts of town with a well-traveled but persistently unlucky trainer named Murray Friedlander. Murray was the first person I'd ever known who garnished a dry martini with a garlic clove. He was also the first man—and last—I ever met who could drink champagne for breakfast and then proceed to have a productive working day.

It was Murray who suggested that I seek out his colleague P. G. Johnson. He said he'd known P.G. for years, since they were both scraping by in Chicago, and that there was no finer man in the game, nor one who would be better able to help me penetrate the Fortune 500–*cum*–Social Register veneer that lay atop Saratoga like the early morning fog. Murray warned me that P.G. could be prickly, and that he didn't suffer fools, gladly or otherwise, but Murray also said he knew the game intimately at every level, and that unlike many of his famously taciturn colleagues, P.G. could and would talk about it.

I'd never met Johnson, but I'd been aware of him since he came east from Chicago in 1961. He was the leading trainer at Aqueduct that fall, his first in New York, which was the equivalent of a ballplayer just up from Triple A leading the league in batting in his rookie season in the majors.

And though we didn't meet, he and I both attended the 1970 Kentucky Derby. He'd entered a horse called Naskra, and stirred a bit of Vietnam-era controversy by attaching a peace symbol to the horse's bridle. I was tempted to bet on Naskra to show support for the gesture—and because Chateaugay's jockey, Braulio Baeza, was riding him—but, in keeping with my notoriously poor judgment, I put my money on Corn off the Cob. Not that it mattered: Naskra ran fourth, with Corn off the Cob well behind him.

But before I could contact P. G. Johnson at Saratoga, I learned that my father had a brain tumor and that immediate surgery would be required. I left the next day. The tumor was malignant. My father died. He was 56. I never did ask him about *Win, Place and Show.*

By the time I got back to Saratoga to write about it, I was sixty. It hadn't occurred to me that P. G. Johnson would still be there.

3 Saratoga Springs is a peaceful old town of twenty-five thousand in upstate New York that for six weeks in summer becomes the one place in America—with the exception of Louisville during Derby Week—where horse racing shows it can still be an obsession.

In 2001, for the first time, more than one million people passed through Saratoga's gates during the thirty-six-day racing season. Poor weather held attendance in the six figures in 2002, but new records—both for the season and for the Travers Day rematch between Funny Cide and Empire Maker—were being proclaimed as sure things for 2003.

Of Saratoga's many unique aspects, this continued success was perhaps the most striking. Notwithstanding that at least once a week attendance figures were inflated by giveaways of T-shirts, tote bags, clocks, mugs, bobblehead dolls, and the like, Saratoga was the only track in the country to have bucked the decades-long decline in attendance that had devastated the sport.

The Saratoga of 2003 might have been hokey rather than hallowed, as much theme park as racetrack, but at least it was there, open six days a week for six weeks, and drawing an average of more than 25,000 spectators per day.

Elsewhere across America, from Aqueduct to Hollywood Park, from Arlington to the Fair Grounds in New Orleans, people were staying away from racetracks in droves. Not only second-tier venues, such as Longacres in Seattle, and New Jersey's Atlantic City, but even the fabled Hialeah had shut down. Other tracks, such as Delaware Park, had survived—if this can be called survival—only by installing slot machines.

Other than Saratoga, only five tracks in America had drawn an average of even 10,000 patrons per day in 2002. These were Churchill Downs and Keeneland, in Kentucky; Oaklawn Park, in Little Rock, Arkansas; and Santa Anita and Del Mar, in Southern California. At Aqueduct, accessible by subway from all parts of New York City, and built to comfortably house crowds of more than 50,000, average daily attendance had fallen below 5,000.

Yogi Berra was reputed to have said about a well-known restaurant, "Nobody goes there anymore. It's too crowded." With racetracks, it was different: Nobody wanted to go anymore because they were too empty.

Statistics compiled by the Jockey Club showed that the amount of money wagered at U.S. Thoroughbred tracks in 2002 had fallen by about 35 percent in seven years, while the sum bet offtrack rose equivalently. People were still betting on horses. They just weren't going to the track to do it, because it was so much easier, and often so much more pleasant, not to go to the track. Virtual reality had overtaken the sound of pounding hooves. And, in the process, the sport had utterly lost its hold on the public imagination.

Two examples might suffice. In the time of the actual Seabiscuit, the 1930s, Hollywood made sixty-eight movies with a horse-racing theme. When it was released in 2003, the movie *Seabiscuit,* based on Laura Hillenbrand's book, was the first Hollywood film about horse racing since Richard Dreyfuss cantered across the screen in *Let It Ride* in 1989.

Even more tellingly, in its first twenty-eight years of publication, *Sports Illustrated* featured the Kentucky Derby on the cover twenty-one times. Since 1983, not a single *Sports Illustrated* cover had been devoted to the Derby.

Dead in the water racing was, and over the past quarter century much has been written in an attempt to explain why. Reasons abound. Among them:

The prices paid for the best-bred yearlings—sometimes climbing above $10 million, as Japanese and Arab money flowed into the game—spurred owners to retire their stakes winners early, because greater profit could be made through procreation than from providing recreation to the masses. Thus, the sport was deprived of its stars.

The increased acceptance by state racing commissions of the use of drugs such as Lasix (a diuretic that could help to control pulmonary bleeding, but which also helped to flush illegal or untested stimulants from the system) and Butazolidin (or "bute," a painkiller and anti-inflammatory medication that made it easier for trainers to race unsound horses) diminished already shaky public confidence in the integrity of the sport.

More and more of the best jockeys—the only human athletes involved in the game—were Hispanic, making them of less interest and less use to American sportswriters and broadcasters. In part this was due to linguistic limitations; in part it was simply racist.

The racetrack and state racing association executives who determined how horse racing would interact with its fan base after television became a household appliance chose, for decades, to not make the sport widely and freely available (in contrast to baseball, for example), thereby keeping racing's appeal secret from at least two generations of potential fans.

The same ruling bodies—and the New York Racing Association, which operates Saratoga, as well as Belmont and Aqueduct, was chief among the offenders—treated their shrinking bands of in-person patrons much the way dogs are treated in a pound: as disposable and not terribly desirable commodities whose presence was more a nuisance than a necessity.

More efficient and faster-paced means of gambling (and not only on horses) became widely available to the common man. First there was off-track betting; then state lotteries; then Atlantic City, which brought casinos into the Northeastern megalopolis; then simulcasting, which enabled bettors to go, not to the shabby old track at the edge of a bad neighborhood but to a snazzy new (heated or air-conditioned) parlor with adequate parking, large-screen television, comfortable chairs, and employees who didn't treat them like dogs; then the spread of Indian casinos; then interactive betting on horses through television and computer.

The horses themselves were not what they used to be. Through most of the twentieth century, as stated in the preface to *Training Thoroughbred Horses*, by fabled trainer Preston Burch, "The horses ran for the sheer joy of running. The elixir which flowed through their veins was nothing more than the heart and courage inherent in the Thoroughbred." The 1992 reprint of Burch's 1953 book points out that "by 1992, the Derby winner took a full second longer to cover the fast track than did the 1953 winner," and that "most of the field ran on Lasix or bute or both." This did not exactly constitute improvement of the breed.

Horses began to acquire stupid names. Where once fans could thrill to the feats of Arts and Letters, Majestic Prince, Damascus, and the like, they eventually were confronted with such excrescences as Easycashfloforutu, Youmakemethorbaby, and Imgunabeinpictures.

Besides all that, most of the people who used to go to the racetrack were dead.

As far back as I could remember, the track had been populated mostly by disreputable, disheveled old white guys who smoked. A lot of them probably even smoked in bed. While drinking cheap whiskey straight from the pint bottle. In rooming houses with stained ceilings and bad plumbing. Where their racking coughs penetrated the thin walls all night long.

Eventually—and what could you expect, given that lifestyle—these guys died. And for all the reasons listed above, and more, no new guys came along to take their place.

The collapse of racing as a spectator sport that drew large crowds for big races, and at least moderate numbers every day, caused many newspapers to drastically reduce or abandon entirely their coverage of it. Not only did generations of potential fans grow up without exposure to the sport, the rising, and later ruling, generation of sportswriters and sports editors in America knew nothing and cared less about racing.

The decline in coverage led to a further erosion of spectator interest, which led to even lower attendance, which eventually rendered funereal the once-effervescent atmosphere of America's finest tracks. By 2003, horse racing was no longer a vibrant part of America's sporting scene, but rather a faded relic of a bygone age. Far more people would go to a movie about a horse that raced more than fifty years earlier than would watch a real horse race.

Saratoga was the one shining exception. Certainly, the champagne had been stirred. The grand old dame had been tarted up in ways that might have made Red Smith and Joe Palmer weep, but with season attendance at the million mark, at least they would have had plenty of shoulders besides each other's to cry on. Saratoga had been the first of America's great racetracks. Now it loomed as the last.

———

The 2003 Saratoga season had people in even more than the usual tizzy. Funny Cide, a Saratoga horse owned by Saratoga people, had won both the Kentucky Derby and the Preakness—the first time a New York–bred had ever done so. In August, in the Travers Stakes, annually the biggest race on the Saratoga calendar, Funny Cide was expected to again confront Empire Maker, who in June had beaten him in the Belmont Stakes to deny him what would have been racing's first Triple Crown in twenty-five years.

Saratoga officials were predicting that the Travers would draw the largest crowd in the track's history, and were talking, for the first time, of opening the infield to spectators, as Churchill Downs did annually on Derby Day, and as Pimlico did for the Preakness.

Adding to the frothy atmosphere was the impending local premiere of the *Seabiscuit* movie, already billed as the popular entertainment that would reignite America's long-dormant passion for the game.

———

My own involvement had reached a peak in the Churchill Downs winner's circle moments after Seattle Slew won the 1977 Kentucky Derby. I was working on a *New York* magazine story about the horse and his jockey, Jean Cruguet, and wound up literally smelling the roses alongside Cruguet's wife. For me, that was the mountaintop. Short of buying my own horse and having it win the Derby, there seemed no way to replicate the experience, and I didn't try.

There was, of course, more to it than that. I got caught up in work that absorbed me so totally that I stopped following not only racing, but all sports. I moved from western New Jersey, where I'd been within a two-hour drive of half a dozen Thoroughbred tracks, to western Massachusetts where, forty-eight weeks a year, I was four hours from the closest. I found myself with five children, a circumstance that profoundly altered my recreational habits. I persuaded myself that I had a better chance of beating the stock market than the track.

Without ever intending to, I drifted away from the racing world. Years passed. I stopped going entirely. I lost touch with my friends from the track. A whole generation of trainers and jockeys slipped away. Calumet Farms went bankrupt. Hialeah shut down. My children grew up and had children of their own. A century ended and a new one began. Like many other things that once had been important to me, racing receded into my past.

Then, in 2001, I noticed that a book about a 1930s race-horse named Seabiscuit was attracting considerable attention, and even selling in large numbers. This seemed, to put it mildly, counterintuitive. Horse racing was dead and gone in America. How could a book about an old-time horse be of such interest to so many?

Reading it—which I did not do until 2003—provided many answers, not the least of which was that Laura Hillenbrand offered an evocative re-creation of a time in America when life was still lived on a human scale, and the future still held more promise than dread. Reading it also reminded me why—beyond an urge to gamble—I'd been drawn to the racetrack in the first place.

In her review in the *New York Review of Books*, Elizabeth Hardwick praised Hillenbrand's "microscopic recreations of every moment" of life as lived at the track. As I read the book, I found myself missing that life for the first time in many years. So much so that in May 2003, for the first time in many years, I watched the telecast of the Kentucky Derby.

I'd read nothing about the race in advance, but as I watched, I recognized the names of two of the trainers: Bobby Frankel and Barclay Tagg.

I remembered both from Saratoga. Frankel had been a brash young Brooklyn-born claiming trainer who seemed to have more winners than friends. There also had been rumors about him pharmaceutically enhancing the performance of some of his runners. Frankel denied all wrongdoing, but amid much whispering in the early seventies, he suddenly decamped for California, where not only the weather but equine drug-testing procedures were considerably more mellow.

He had come far since those days. He was now training for both a Saudi Arabian prince and an American almost-billionaire. In 2002, he was the country's leading money-winning trainer, and in the 2003 Derby he was starting not only the favorite, Empire Maker, but the second choice, Peace Rules.

I remembered Barclay Tagg as a rider of steeplechase horses—the ones that jump over hedges and sometimes land on their feet. He had apparently been a relatively unsuccessful trainer in Maryland and Pennsylvania for many years. Funny Cide was the first Derby entrant of his career, and was said to have only a modest prospect of success.

Funny Cide was a gelding—he'd been castrated—and had been bred in New York, which had never produced a Derby winner. He was owned, the story went, by a bunch of guys from upstate New York who'd drunk a few beers at a high school reunion a couple of years earlier and had decided to go partners on a horse. They were apparently Saratoga regulars, though a social cut or two below the blue bloods.

The events of the day are by now quite familiar: Funny Cide won the race, at 12-1. Bobby Frankel's horses ran second and third. Barclay Tagg squirmed under the unaccustomed spotlight. The owners, a splendidly unpretentious bunch who had ridden a yellow school bus to the track, became media darlings. They promised that the 2003 Saratoga meet would be a madcap party from start to finish, with Funny Cide, a hometown hero, the star of the show.

It had been four years since I'd last published a book, and thirty-two years since I'd gone to Saratoga with the intention of writing a book about a racing season there. I had no idea whom or what I might find, but I decided it was time to go back—time to do what my father's sudden illness and death had forced me to leave undone in 1971.

———

I arrived on the morning of Monday, July 21, 2003, two days before the racing began. The air was heavy with humidity, and showers fell at regular intervals. There were as many horse vans as cars on the streets. I had rented a tiny cottage, walking distance from the track. The cottage had been vacated only hours earlier by a couple of Skidmore College students, and the landlord was still pulling empty beer bottles from under the couch.

I was paying $8,500 for the six-week season, a price that might have been a bargain on Martha's Vineyard, but seemed steep for thirty miles north of Albany, when calculated on the basis of square footage times distance-from-the-nearest-ocean times intensity-of-lingering-stale-beer-smell times percentage-of-furniture-that-was-plastic.

Leaving my bags in the custody of my sweaty, grunting landlord—who insisted on an additional $1,000 security deposit—I took a stroll along Broadway. It was the town's only main street, but a fine one. I was twenty-eight the first time I came to Saratoga to write a book about it. Now, I was sixty. Rip Van Winkle flashes were unavoidable.

Had it been possible to get past the Funny Cide and Seabiscuit paraphernalia, Broadway probably would have looked much as I remembered it. But that wasn't possible. One encountered the name "Funny Cide" approximately one hundred times per block. Broadway was emblazoned with Funny Cide posters, store windows were stuffed with Funny Cide merchandise, and a Funny Cide obelisk had been erected in front of City Hall.

Markets were advertising a beer called Funny Cide Lite, and announcing the impending arrival of wines called Funny Cide Red and Funny Cide White. A brand-new Funny Cide street sign stood at the intersection of Union and East streets, and on Caroline Street, the "official" Funny Cide store had opened its doors. Newspapers from both Saratoga Springs and Albany carried front-page stories about the epidemic of "Funny Cide Fever" that was raging unchecked in the area.

It was a virulent strain: Funny Cide caps and scarves all but jumped on my head and wrapped themselves around my neck, while Funny Cide umbrellas thrust themselves into my hand, and Funny Cide bumper stickers fought to affix themselves to my car.

Seabiscuit was running a close second. Virtually every type of Seabiscuit-related contrivance short of a sex toy was for sale on Broadway, although Seabiscuit had run only three times at Saratoga, and never in a race of distinction. The *Seabiscuit* film would premiere at the National Museum of Racing, across the street from the track, on Wednesday night, providing the conclusion to Saratoga's opening day. Even at $150 a ticket, the event had been sold out for weeks.

Rain chased me back to my cottage. On its sagging mini-porch, a dozen large plastic garbage bags stood like sentinels, presumably awaiting further disposal. After a couple of hours, during which I was able to observe that no matter how hard it rained, at least the roof didn't leak, I ventured out again, this time to Union Avenue, the gracious boulevard of tall shade trees and grand old Victorian houses that leads to the main gate of the track.

En route, my eye was caught by the first poster I had seen all day that didn't advertise either Funny Cide or Seabiscuit. It stood in front of the National Museum of Racing and announced that the public would be welcome that evening to hear talks by a small group of racing notables, including the estimable jockey Richard Migliore and trainer P. G. Johnson.

Though he'd come into the game after I left, I was aware

that Migliore (who would win the 2004 Florida Derby aboard long shot Friends Lake) had been a successful and respected rider in New York for more than twenty years. I also had read that a number of the sons of trainers who'd been prominent at Saratoga in the early 1970s—trainers such as Allen Jerkens, Del Carroll, Johnny Campo, Angel Penna—were trying to follow in their fathers' footsteps, with varying degrees of success. I assumed that, despite the lack of a "Jr." after the name, the "P. G. Johnson" who would speak that night was one of these.

I skipped the event in favor of dinner with friends. I'd have ample opportunity in the next six weeks to chat with Migliore, and perhaps even to introduce myself to this presumed son of the fabled P. G. Johnson, and to ask him how his father had fared in later years.

The next day, I had lunch with Pierre Bellocq. He was the only person I knew from the old days who was still actively connected to the game. It was Pierre who had made housemates of Murray Friedlander and me, but it had been more than twenty years since I shared a meal with him.

As a teenager in France during World War II, Pierre had exercised horses at Maisons-Laffitte. In America, where he'd moved in the early 1950s, he was known professionally as "PEB." He'd been drawing caricatures and cartoons for the *Daily Racing Form* and its predecessor, the *Morning Tele-*

graph, for forty-nine years. He was a man of immense talent, charm, and generosity, both renowned and beloved throughout the racing world.

During the 1960s, he and I both worked at the *Philadelphia Inquirer,* Pierre as editorial cartoonist and myself as a columnist. For the next ten years, even after we'd both left the newspaper, Pierre guided me through many a barn and into numerous jockeys' rooms around the country. As I moved away from racing—and, eventually, moved three thousand miles from Pierre's base in Princeton, New Jersey—we lost touch with each other.

The lunch was as festive as Pierre's plan to drive back to Princeton later in the afternoon would permit. He brought me up to date on his family—two of his sons were in racing, one as a trainer and the other as executive director of the national Horsemen's Benevolent and Protective Association—and on dozens of people about whom I'd heard nothing in a quarter century, and he familiarized me with the names of many who had more recently risen to prominence.

Eventually, I mentioned that I had passed up a chance to listen to the son of P. G. Johnson the night before.

"The son?" he said. "No, no, P.G. does not have a son. He has two daughters, and one of them works for the *Racing Form,* but I am quite sure he does not have a son."

"Then who was that speaking last night?"

"That was Mr. P.G. himself."

"You mean P. G. Johnson—the real P. G. Johnson—is still training horses?"

"My friend," Pierre said, "you have been sleeping under a rock for much too long. P. G. Johnson is not only still a trainer, he is now in the Hall of Fame, he holds the record for most consecutive years of winning a race here at Saratoga—I think it is now more than forty—and, of course, he now has a big horse.

"He has Volponi. He is not only the trainer, but the owner."

"Volponi?"

"You don't know even Volponi? Now, you must be joking. Last year at Arlington Park he wins the biggest race of all—the Breeders' Cup Classic. This race is worth 4 million dollars, and Volponi is the longest shot in it, more than 40-1, and he wins by the most lengths in the history of the race, and Mr. P.G. becomes the oldest trainer ever to win the Classic. Really, you do not know this story?"

"Pierre, I haven't heard the name P. G. Johnson for at least twenty-five years. And he was no kid when I was here the last time."

"Well, he is no kid now, but he is, I would say, the grand old man of racing, like Sunny Jim Fitzsimmons fifty years ago."

"Murray Friedlander told me in 1971 that I should meet him."

"Murray was right, but it is even more important now. I think the best way—so he won't chase you away—is through his daughter from the *Racing Form*. You should call Charlie Hayward and ask him to contact her."

Charlie Hayward was an old acquaintance from the world of book publishing who had become president of the *Daily Racing Form*. Pierre gave me his phone number. I called him that night. He called P. G. Johnson's daughter. Within a few days, she had arranged for me to go to the barn and meet her father. Which was why the first thing he'd said to me was that I must have been the guy he was supposed to be nice to so his daughter wouldn't lose her goddamned job.

SKIP DICKSTEIN

P.G. receiving the Breeders' Cup

4 **In 1997, when he was inducted into the Hall of Fame at the National Museum of Racing in Saratoga, P. G. Johnson had joked about never having had a big horse.**

"I was told a few years ago that I needed a big horse to get here," he said. "So I ran out with a tape measurement, to the barn." He said he measured all his horses, and it was true. "I didn't have a big horse."

The comment prompted a wave of laughter.

To racing people, the term "big horse" describes not size, but accomplishment. By that standard, Man o' War has been the biggest horse of all. Citation and Native Dancer and Secretariat were huge, as were Count Fleet and War Admiral, and, of course, Seabiscuit. More recently, Seattle Slew and Affirmed and Spectacular Bid have been very big horses, along with the geldings Kelso, Forego, John Henry, and Cigar, and—not to be forgotten—the awesome, electrifying, and doomed filly Ruffian.

Since P. G. Johnson had begun his training career at Lincoln Fields in Crete, Illinois, in 1943, many hundreds of Thoroughbreds had earned the appellation of "big horse."

But despite winning more than three thousand races over the years, P.G. had never had one.

In 1973, he won the Hollywood Derby with Amen II.

In 1977, he sent out Quiet Little Table to beat horse of the year Forego in the Suburban Handicap at Belmont Park.

In 1983, he was the leading trainer at Saratoga in races won.

Over the winter of 1987–88, he won twelve consecutive stakes races at tracks in New York, New Jersey, and Maryland.

In 1988, he trained Maplejinsky to a victory in the Alabama Stakes, Saratoga's—and America's—oldest and most prestigious race for fillies.

In 1996, he won the Sword Dancer Handicap at Saratoga with Kiri's Clown.

These were fine and noble animals, but by P.G.'s own reckoning none had quite been a big horse.

Despite more than a half century in the game, he had never trained the winner of a Triple Crown or Breeders' Cup event.

And in 1999, when the *Blood-Horse* magazine chose the top one hundred Thoroughbred racehorses of the twentieth century, none of P.G.'s made the list.

He'd come to racing not from the bluegrass country of Kentucky, nor from the posh polo clubs and horse-show venues that dotted the mid-Atlantic states, but from the gritty sidewalks of Chicago: a bare-knuckled, blue-collar kid who had both ambition and attitude.

Although he operated only a public stable, and never trained for the Social Register types who occupied the upper echelons of the sport in New York—and whose expensive horses, more often than not, won the most lucrative and prestigious races at Aqueduct, Belmont, and Saratoga—he was among New York's top ten trainers in races won throughout the 1960s.

His horses were cheap and his turnover high. He competed mostly in claiming races, in which, for a predetermined price, any horse entered can be bought (that is, "claimed") by any other registered owner on the grounds.

These pedestrian events provided most of the grist for America's racing mills. Three quarters of the races run in the United States were claiming races, and the operative principle was no different from that which governed Wall Street: Buy low, sell high. But because, unlike the stock market, this aspect of horse racing was essentially a zero-sum game, and because the purses offered in claiming races were so low, and because the trainer received only 10 percent of the purse, life at the claiming level was both frenetic and very thinly insulated by margin for error.

From the start, P.G. established himself—as he previously had done in Chicago—as a sharp-elbowed, sharp-tongued practitioner of this unglamorous craft, with an especially keen eye for the potential pearl in a herd of swine.

He flourished in the age of the trainer as *auteur,* not CEO, when men of quirky personality and arcane craftsmanship dominated the game. His peers were horsemen like Elliot Burch, Max Hirsch, Allen Jerkens, Tommy Kelly, Horatio Luro, Mack Miller, Eddie Neloy, John Nerud, Angel Penna, Scotty Schulhofer, Woody Stephens, Charlie Whittingham, and Bill Winfrey.

That era came to an end in the late 1980s as megatrainers (at first, D. Wayne Lukas; later Bob Baffert and Bobby Frankel; and more recently, Steve Asmussen) brought a Wal-Mart mindset to the business, overwhelming by sheer force of numbers. This new, entrepreneurial breed managed hundreds of horses for dozens of owners simultaneously, building vast equine empires on which the sun never set.

The training style of P. G. Johnson ("I only want to train what I can see every morning"), in which patience was considered the cardinal virtue, and young horses were not pressed to show profit before they were strong enough to withstand racing's rigors, became as anachronistic as the independent bookseller in the era of Borders and Barnes & Noble.

———

Years earlier, however, P.G. had come to realize that maintaining a medium-sized public stable—thirty to forty horses at any one time—for owners of moderate means simply was not enough to provide financial security for his family. The only honest path to profit for a hands-on trainer like himself was through breeding and ownership.

He barely broke even on the fees he charged for stabling and training, and given his paucity of stakes-level horses, his trainer's share of 10 percent of the purse did not tip the balance appreciably. In the mid-1970s, for example, even in New York, a typical claiming race might offer a $9,000 purse, of which half went to the owner of the winner, with smaller fractions paid to those whose horses finished second through fifth. Thus, third place in the fifth race at Saratoga might have been worth $120 to the trainer. It took many such finishes to pay the mortgage in Rockville Centre and send two daughters to college.

Not being in a position to make seven-figure purchases at the Saratoga or Keeneland yearling sales, P.G. began buying inexpensive broodmares whose lineage he liked, and breeding them to stallions whose stud fees he could afford.

For years, P.G. had been developing breeding theories based on principles articulated by Federico Tesio, the fabled Italian who produced two of the greatest horses of the first half of the twentieth century—Ribot and Nearco.

"Tesio's choice of stallions was based on economics and energy," P.G. would later say. "Since he couldn't afford a leading sire, he would look to a stallion of almost equal credentials, who had been unimpressive in his first two crops. The theory being that he could get to him cheaper after two bad years, which could have been the result of energy depleted at the track. Renewed energy plus low stud fee equals success.

"In terms of mares, he always chose well-bred mares with little or no racing ability. Again: economics."

Although he continued to operate P. G. Johnson Stable Inc., he focused increasingly on training and racing his own horses for his family's new venture, Amherst Stable, named after the Long Island street on which they lived.

This proved prescient, because the era of the megatrainer eventually cast smaller-scale, hands-on trainers such as P.G. into the shadows. By the mid-1990s, both his annual earnings from training and his percentage of races won had declined sharply.

In 1997, the year of his induction into the Hall of Fame, P.G.'s horses earned less than $500,000 in purse money, of which his share as trainer was less than $50,000. By contrast,

Wayne Lukas, the year's leader, had winnings of more than $10 million.

But by then Amherst Stable was flourishing. In an era of $10 million yearlings, P.G. never paid more than $30,000 for a horse. But he burrowed deeply into the arcane world of pedigree analysis, and, over time, developed confidence in his ability to spot a bargain bloodline.

His approach was to buy broodmares whose ancestry indicated potential, even if their own performance on the racetrack did not. He then mated his mares to affordable stallions whose own families hailed, more or less, from the right side of the Thoroughbred tracks.

And then he hoped for the best. As a hedge, he often sold stakes of up to 50 percent in his newborn foals, choosing partners whom he trusted not to try to interfere with his training methods. Unlike many of his higher-volume colleagues, who were under constant pressure to produce quick returns, P.G. did not risk breaking his young horses down by rushing them to the races too soon. As both trainer and breeder, he was a tortoise on a track populated increasingly by large, hungry hares.

At the Saratoga sale in the summer of 1993, he bought a daughter of Dancing Party for $8,000. He named the filly Prom Knight. She raced only once before being injured and then retired. Over the next few years, however, P.G. became increasingly intrigued by the caliber and ancestry of her European sire, an Irish Derby winner named Sir Harry Lewis.

In 1997, he paid $20,000 to have her bred to Cryptoclearance, a stakes-winning grandson of the brilliant Hoist the Flag, who was, in turn, a son of the superb Tom Rolfe. Hoist the Flag and Tom Rolfe were the sort of horses P.G. had never been given an opportunity to train, but now, as a breeder and owner, he was able to buy into their families.

In April 1998, at Parrish Hill Farm in Lexington, Kentucky, Prom Knight gave birth to a healthy foal. After more than a half century in the game, P.G. was about to have a big horse.

———

In Italian, the phrase *vecchio volpone* means "sly old fox." In 1999, a former Rikers Island social worker turned journalist and aspiring fiction writer, Paul Volponi (in 2002, Black Heron Press of Seattle would publish his first novel, *Rikers*), wrote a column for an industry newsletter called the *New York Thoroughbred Observer* in which he named P.G. the winner of his annual "Volponi Award," in recognition of the year's craftiest—as in sly fox—performance by a trainer.

Volponi the writer cited as the basis for the award P.G.'s having won five races with horses coming back from long layoffs. In appreciation, although he'd never met Paul Volponi, P.G. named the Cryptoclearance–Prom Knight colt after him.

He also sold a 50 percent share in the horse to a Long Island accountant named Ed Baier, who had been an occasional partner for years.

From birth, Volponi the horse was rough and ungainly. At one point, the farm manager in Ocala even suggested castrating him, but P.G., with an eye toward future breeding potential, instructed that the colt be kept intact.

Volponi made his first start at Belmont in June 2000, when he was two, finishing third in a race restricted to maidens, the racing term for horses that have never won a race. Volponi didn't win any of his next three starts, either.

Nonetheless, on October 22 at Belmont, his crafty old fox of a trainer switched Volponi from a dirt surface to grass and raced him at a distance greater than a mile for the first time. The race was a minor stakes called the Pilgrim. It was unusual to enter a horse who'd not yet won any kind of race in a stakes, the highest level of competition, but even at age seventy-five, P.G. remained sharply intuitive.

At odds of 10-1, Volponi came from behind to win the Pilgrim. The victory, combined with two seconds and two thirds in his previous four races, raised Volponi's earnings to almost $100,000, and P.G. gave him the rest of the year off.

Through much of the following year, Volponi was a disappointment. In his first seven starts, he won only once, and finished a dull seventh in the Travers at Saratoga, at 13-1. Then, almost a year to the day after his triumph in the 2000

Pilgrim, Volponi won the Pegasus Handicap at New Jersey's Meadowlands, returning $150,000 to owners Johnson and Baier. More significantly, the victory enabled P.G. to sell the $8,000 dam, Prom Knight, for $425,000.

In July 2002, as a four-year-old, Volponi won the Poker Handicap at Belmont. Like the Pilgrim Stakes, the race was contested on grass. In the United States, unlike Europe, grass is a less common racing surface than dirt. Throughout his career, P.G. had been considered especially masterful at training horses to run on grass, and, after the Poker, he decided that this less jarring terrain would prove the path of least resistance for the heavy, hard-running Volponi.

P.G., however, failed to explain this to the horse. Volponi lost three races in a row on the turf. At Saratoga, he finished second in the Bernard Baruch and third in the Sword Dancer. And even though P.G. installed the more experienced Jose Santos in place of Volponi's heretofore regular rider, Shaun Bridgmohan, and even though he was the 4-5 favorite, Volponi managed only a second in the September Breeders' Cup Handicap at Belmont.

At that point, the path of least resistance seemed back across the Hudson River to New Jersey. But on October 4, despite a return to both dirt and the Meadowlands, Volponi was a beaten favorite once again.

P.G. then faced a decision. On Saturday, October 26, the

national Breeders' Cup—North American racing's most consequential event—would be contested. For the first time in the nineteen-year history of the event, the races would be run at Arlington Park, in P.G.'s old hometown of Chicago. And, for the first time, P.G. thought he had a horse worth entering. The question was, in which race?

The Breeders' Cup program comprises eight races, each intended to determine the year's best horse in a particular category: from two-year-old fillies sprinting three quarters of a mile on dirt, to older horses (many of them European) running a mile and a half on grass. Purses for individual races range from $1 million to $4 million.

On October 9, which happened to be his seventy-seventh birthday, P.G. paid $27,500 to pre-enter Volponi in the one-mile turf race, and another $27,500 to keep him eligible for the day's most lucrative and prestigious event, the one-and-a-quarter-mile Breeders' Cup Classic.

Throughout Volponi's three-year, twenty-two-race career, P.G. had tinkered with the horse like either a Swiss watchmaker or mad scientist, depending on one's point of view. He'd tried five different jockeys on Volponi, moved him back and forth between grass and dirt seven times, and raced him at seven different distances on dirt and five on grass, and at five different tracks. Point of view, of course, was largely determined by how much money one had won or lost by betting on Volponi. Given that the horse had lost eight of the ten races in which he'd been favored, those in the Swiss-watchmaker camp were few.

It would cost an additional $15,000 to actually start Volponi in the Breeders' Cup Mile, while the Classic would require an additional $40,000 payment. But the Classic offered a $4 million purse—four times that of the Mile. And there was another factor. Twice in the previous year and a half, P.G. had been operated on for prostate cancer. At seventy-seven, and weakened by the radiation treatments that had followed the surgery, he realized that this return to Chicago would not be simply a homecoming, but, in all likelihood, a last hurrah.

He entered Volponi in the Classic

How unrealistic this seemed was illustrated almost immediately by the Arlington Park oddsmaker, who put the horse at 50-1 in the morning line, making him the longest shot in the field. The favorite was Bobby Frankel's Medaglia d'Oro, who had won both the Travers and the Jim Dandy at Saratoga after having run second in the Belmont Stakes. Also strongly backed were the year's Kentucky Derby and Preakness winner, War Emblem; Evening Attire, who had won the Saratoga Breeders' Cup Handicap and the Jockey Club Gold Cup at Belmont; the California champion Came Home; and Hawk Wing, shipping in from Ireland for renowned European trainer Aidan O'Brien.

By post time, it was clear that bettors also considered the six other starters to be more likely than Volponi to win the race. P.G.'s last best hope was sent off at 43-1, highest odds on the board.

Part of the extraordinary drama inherent in a major horse race arises from the awareness—shared by owners, trainers, jockeys, and all others involved except the horses— that so much of import will be determined in such a short space of time.

A baseball game lasts nine innings, a soccer match ninety minutes, a championship tennis match no less than three sets. Though moments of intense excitement and spectacular achievement become what is remembered about each, the climax is preceded by a variety of ebbs and flows, by multiple shifts in momentum, and often even by moments of tedium.

Not so in a horse race. From the instant the bell goes off and the front panels of the starting gate spring open, time, and life itself, seem suspended.

The animals surge forward at the start like water pouring over a falls, quickly forming themselves into a moving stream, wider in some spots than others, but flowing forward at what seems a constant rate.

Should one have a stake in the outcome—whether it be a simple matter of money, or something more complex and mysterious, such as a hope or a dream—one's heart is in one's mouth from start to finish. Adrenaline floods the bloodstream, the pulse races, the skin either tingles or grows cold, and strange noises, ranging from abject whimpers to blood-curdling screams, escape from one's mouth. The race is over in a millisecond but takes a lifetime to run. And no matter the result, there can be no going back, and life will never be quite the same.

Though disqualification, on rare occasions, may alter the official order of finish, there are no second chances in racing: What's done is done. The tantalizing, titillating future—so fraught with promise, potential, and the smell of red roses in the spring—is suddenly the past: no less than a lasting memory, no more than an inalterable line in a record book that stretches back to the dawn of time.

That's a lot to have happen in 122 seconds, the length of time one might spend stopped at a traffic light.

But in a fraction of a second less than that, in the gathering dusk at the end of a cold and blustery Chicago afternoon, Volponi rewarded P.G. with the biggest victory of his sixty-year career, beating Medaglia d'Oro by six and a half lengths. It was the biggest winning margin in the history of the race. And, paying $89 for every two dollars bet on him to win, Volponi became the second-longest-priced horse ever to triumph in the race. More to the point for P.G., the winner's share of the purse was $2,080,000.

Considerable glory also was involved. By having trained a

Breeders' Cup Classic winner, P.G. joined the company of such men as Lukas, Whittingham, Neil Drysdale, Sonny Hine, Bill Mott, Jack Van Berg, and Carl Nafzger, and accomplished something that neither Bobby Frankel, nor Todd Pletcher, nor P.G.'s old friend and fellow Hall of Famer Allen Jerkens had ever done.

Even more satisfying, as Volponi's breeder and owner, P.G. joined ranks populated by any number of men and women who, for reasons ranging from dislike of his sharp tongue and independence to blatant anti-Semitism, never would have hired him as a trainer.

But what pleased P.G. most was that it had happened back home in Chicago. As a self-described "punk" from the city's prewar North Side—and remembering that during his earliest years as a trainer he couldn't even get stall space at Arlington Park—he was especially delighted that it was at Arlington that he became the oldest trainer ever to win a Breeders' Cup event.

Inevitably, many newspapers the next day described the outcome as a Hollywood ending. In the era of *Seabiscuit,* this was not merely an empty cliché, as Disney soon demonstrated by optioning the movie rights to the story of P.G.'s life.

The young P.G.

P.G. I was born in Chicago on October 9, 1925. My mother died giving birth. I didn't have any brothers or sisters. My father was a vaudeville musician, playing the Chicago Theater, downtown on State Street, and the Terminal Theater on the West Side.

He worked for Balaban and Katz, the people that owned the biggest chain of theaters in the United States. Barney Balaban and Sam Katz. Balaban wound up running Paramount and Katz wound up running MGM. My father was a drummer in the pit. Every week they showed a movie, there was *Movietone News,* there was a cartoon, and there was a stage show, with every famous person that ever lived.

Two of my father's best friends were the Duncan Sisters. They did blackface. They took the show *Topsy and Eva* on the road. "Ah didn't do nothin'. That white man put me in the bed." That kind of stuff. I loved when they were in town because they gave me a dollar. He'd take it away and give me a quarter, but that was still a lot of money.

I'd go backstage every day after school and stay until the show was over. I was supposed to do my homework, but I'd fall asleep, and eventually my father thought that that was not doing me any good, so he sent me to live with his sister, her husband, and their two kids. Her husband wore a yarmulke all the time. I have never yet met a rottener son of a bitch, and I've met some bad people.

I lived with them for maybe a year. When we ate, we couldn't talk at the table. One day we were mumbling something and he meant to say, "Eat! Don't talk!" but he said, "Talk! Don't eat!" and I couldn't stop laughing. I was sitting next to that son of a bitch and he whacked me, and he had a ring on, and it cut me.

That was Friday. My father came the next day. The first thing he said was, "What happened to Sonny?"—he called me Sonny—"Has he been fighting again?" And my aunt said, "Dave hit him. Accidentally." Where was Dave, my father says. He was in the shul or something. He wasn't around. My father threw my clothes in the back of the car and I was gone. Never went back. He took me to live with him at the Rogers Park Hotel.

He was playing at the Uptown Theater at the time, which was a big theater, on the borderline of Evanston. Balaban and Katz had two theaters up there, the Uptown and the Granada, and he played both those, and he was also still playing at the Terminal Theater, which was near the hotel.

But he says, "I can't leave you alone all the time, that's no good." Down Sheridan Road going south—I don't think it was two miles from the hotel—was a place called the Sherwood School for Boys. Not a reform school, a boarding school. I was there about a week. I could not stand it. I couldn't fucking stand it.

Now, I wasn't too smart. You don't wind up on the racetrack if you're too smart. So I told them one day I got a stomachache. The nurse took my temperature; I didn't have a fever. So she says, "Where does it hurt?" I said, "Down here." I didn't know. It didn't hurt anywhere, so how the hell should I know where it hurt?

She called my father, and he comes right over and he says, "Where does it hurt?" Now, I've already established the position, and I can't back away from it even though I'm thinking this is bad. So he makes a call from the school to a doctor he knew, Dr. Ellwood, who says, "Bring him right over. It sounds like appendicitis." Dr. Ellwood pokes my stomach, and he goes, "Harry, we got to get him to the hospital right away. He's got appendicitis, and I've got to get it out of there before it breaks."

Now, I don't know appendicitis from that spittoon over there, but it doesn't sound good to go to a hospital—I still hate 'em—and I know that whatever appendicitis is, I ain't got it, because my stomach don't even hurt. Anyway, my father, being a good Jew, says, "What'll it cost?" The doctor says, "Harry, don't worry about that. We gotta get him there." Next thing I know I got a gown on. Then I'm flat on my back and there's big lights coming down, and "Count to ten backwards with this mask on."

That's how I got out of the Sherwood School for Boys. My father never let me go back because he blamed them for my appendicitis. So I got to go to the public school in Rogers Park, and I got my dog, Yippy, a Kerry Blue terrier. He was great. We'd go down to the beach where the rocks are, along Lake Michigan, and we had a wonderful time, but it was Yippy that damn near ruined my life.

I could stay with my father now, because he had seen the writing on the wall. He had rented some space across the street, and he had started taking pictures of people: portraits. For free, because he wanted to learn. He had these big German lenses he had bought secondhand. I said, "Why are you doing this?" He says, "Because the movie companies have bought the theaters. The double feature is coming. It's all over for vaudeville."

He was looking to get out, and he got lucky. He took a picture of one of the chorus girls at the State-Lake Theater, and she sent the picture to an agent in Hollywood. She turned out to be Betty Grable, and my father became a famous portrait photographer in Chicago. Every formal picture you ever saw of Mayor Daley and all the useless politicians—the portraits and the wedding pictures, the ones like that—my father took them.

Like all musicians, you were either a drunk or you were a horse bettor or you were both, and he was a horse bettor. He would read the entries for Monday's races a month ago, and he would handicap the first and second, say at Belmont, and at Arlington, wherever, and have me look up the results. If he had a winner, I'd circle it. He taught me how to read the *Racing Form,* and to read results. He also started to get the *Turf and Sport Digest,* which had systems in it. He was always trying to devise a system to beat the races. And that sparked my interest a little bit.

But then the awfulest thing in my life happened. After school, I'd come home to the hotel, and I did my homework every day, because if I didn't do good my father was going to put me back in the Sherwood School. This one day it was hot, and I had the door to the apartment open, and Yippy's laying down by my feet, and I'm reading some sort of schoolbook, and the guy who delivers the dry cleaning walks right in.

Well, you couldn't do that with Yippy protecting me. Yippy nailed him. He got him in the calf, got him hard. Blood all over the place. And this guy, you'd think a tiger got him. He threw the cleaning down and ran out of there. The way it turned out, if Yippy would've killed him it would've been better.

My father comes home and there's blood all over the floor, so I had to tell him what happened, and what does a Jewish person think of, first thing? He's gonna get sued. So my father finds out who the guy is, the delivery guy, and where he lives. The guy's name was Leonard Goldberg. My father goes over, hat in hand, to the Goldbergs' house, and he meets this guy Leonard's older sister.

Now, my mother's maiden name was Goldberg, and I guess that must have meant something to my father, because he married her. This Goldberg's sister wound up being my stepmother, and she became the bane of my life. She was as rotten as my uncle was, but she had bigger balls.

Once they got married, we had to move. To a bigger, fancier place, that's the kind of woman she was. We moved to the Belmont Hotel, 3100 Belmont Avenue North, and my father took a studio for his photography at 57 East Oak Street, three quarters of a block from Michigan Avenue, across the street from the Drake Hotel.

I couldn't bring Yippy, because the Belmont Hotel was too classy. Besides, after he'd bit her brother in the leg, my new stepmother wasn't going to be any fan of Yippy. We had to give him away, and I was depressed. Just from my step-mother, I was depressed, and then I had to get rid of my dog, which made me a lot more depressed. They didn't have a pill for depression in those days, but I was depressed.

I was about thirteen, still in grade school. In fact, it was in a kid's car right outside the Louis B. Nettelhorst School on North Broadway in East Lake View where I listened to the Seabiscuit–War Admiral match race.

After that, I got real interested in horse racing. My father had done it before, but now I started to buy used *Racing Forms*, used *Turf Flash, Green Sheets, Turf and Sport Digest,* anything I could get my hands on that was specifically about horse racing.

But my interest was different from my father's. I wasn't trying to find a betting system: I wanted to train the horses. From the time I heard the Seabiscuit match race on the radio, I had no ambition in the world other than to be a trainer.

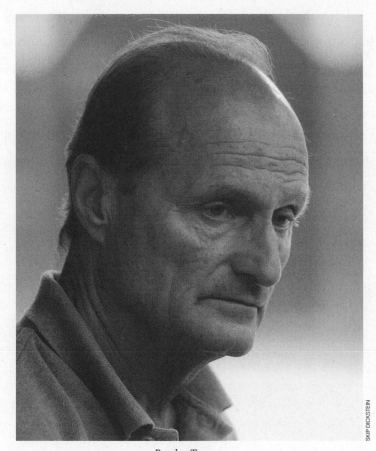

Barclay Tagg

SKIP DICKSTEIN

5   "The trainer: troubled days and nights, considerations obscure and heavy with consequence; the daily judgment of the ground of the track, the bones, aches, and moods of the horse, the wizened souls of the jockeys . . . race after race, anxiety," Elizabeth Hardwick has written.

Add to that the all-consuming, predawn-to-dusk hours; the months, often years, without vacation; the potential for heartbreak, so often realized; the financial insecurity, the physical danger; the precariousness of a career built on the fragile legs of the Thoroughbred and forever at the mercy of faithless owners' whims, and it's a wonder that anyone would choose such a life.

No one does, of course: It chooses them. It also imposes on them a lifetime of discipline, self-reliance, resourcefulness, anxiety, wariness, skepticism, mistrust, discouragement, and incessant fretting about detail.

To the question of what a trainer actually does, one might respond that it would be easier to describe what a trainer does not do. Certainly, such a list would be shorter.

As described on the Web site of Miami's Calder Race

Course, "The trainer teaches horses how to race, hones their speed, builds their endurance, sees to their care, and calls in help to heal their injuries. The trainer [also] selects the races in which the horses will compete."

The trainer is, essentially, the coach of an athletic team, all of whose members are high-strung potential killers, and none of whom can speak.

The trainer decides what his horses should eat and when they should eat it and how much he's willing to pay for it, and from which supplier he should obtain it; what sort of shoes his horses should wear and which blacksmith should be hired to put them on and take them off; what sort of workout— walking, galloping, or running hard—each horse should have each day; how often and against what sort of competition and on what surface and at what distance and at what track each horse should race; which jockey should be employed to ride which horse; how often the horses' teeth should be checked; what blood tests should be performed on which horses and how often, and what laboratory should be used to interpret them; what sort of preventive medications the horses should be given; what treatment they should receive for sore hooves, or ankles or knees or shins; how much the exercise riders and grooms should be paid; how much responsibility should be delegated to which assistant; which horses need additional schooling in the starting gate or paddock; when the veterinarian should be called; what sort of bit should be placed in the horse's mouth; what sort of additional equipment, such as blinkers, should be used; and at least 999 other things that have to be attended to daily, plus whatever else should arise, and that's not counting emergencies.

No one at Saratoga in 2003 seemed to better exemplify the mental and emotional strain the profession could impose and the psychological toll it could take than the veteran Pennsylvania horseman in charge of Funny Cide, Barclay Tagg.

The horse arrived from Belmont in fine shape on Tuesday morning, July 22, the day before the season began. Tagg also arrived on Tuesday morning. He, however, seemed anything but fine, despite—or maybe because of—being back at Saratoga with the first big horse of his life.

"Saratoga's a pain in the neck," he said, grousing about the lack of security in the stable area. "People are wandering in and out all the time." He said he'd be putting up chains to keep the public away from his horse. He added that he hadn't liked making the horse run three hard races in five weeks, and that nothing of the sort would happen again.

"The Triple Crown is over. I don't have to do anything I don't want to now," he said, grimacing as if his personal experience of Funny Cide Fever had left him feeling that on the whole he would have preferred dengue.

Tagg seemed an appealing guy. He was cynical, pessimistic, dour, irritable, sardonic, acerbic, and hot-tempered: all the qualities I most admire in a man. "You can't help the personality God has given you," a trainer who'd known Tagg for many years once explained, but there were those who thought that Tagg could have tried a little harder.

———

I soon learned that, like P. G. Johnson and Allen Jerkens, who turned out to be two of his better friends, Tagg was held in the highest professional esteem by his peers. I lost count of the number of times I heard him described as "a horseman's horseman." But, like Murray Friedlander a generation before him, Tagg had spent most of his career slogging through a bog of misfortune. His pessimism had been honed on experience. He had enjoyed scant success before Funny Cide and he didn't mind letting people know it.

Raised in suburban Philadelphia, Tagg's first exposure to horses had come from horse shows. That background led him to a short career as a steeplechase rider (which was how I remembered him from Saratoga in 1971), but he gave up on that because, as he put it, "I never had any good horses." Those he acquired as a trainer on the Maryland-Pennsylvania circuit for the next twenty years were not much better. It took him twenty-three years to win a Grade I stakes race, and they were not years of lavish lifestyle.

It wasn't until 2001, divorced and with his children grown, that Tagg moved from the minor-league Maryland circuit to New York. Unburdened by a large stable or an imposing reputation, but known for impeccable integrity, Tagg seemed to the partners who would soon own Funny Cide to be the right sort of trainer for their low-budget, small-scale approach. "I asked them one time what made them hire me," Tagg recalled to writer Dale Keiger, "and they said, 'Well, we called two trainers, and you're the one who called back.' "

Tagg spotted Funny Cide—a $20,000 yearling—on a farm in Florida. He paid $75,000 to buy the colt for his new owners, who called themselves Sackatoga Stable. That had been one Kentucky Derby, one Preakness, and almost $2 million ago. Yet Tagg arrived in Saratoga utterly depleted by his bout with success. P. G. Johnson's big horse had given P.G. a new lease on life, but Barclay Tagg's seemed to have plunged Barclay even deeper into gloom.

His moroseness was drawing almost as much comment as his horse. Asked how it felt to win the Kentucky Derby, he replied, "Well, it makes you feel like maybe the whole thirty years wasn't wasted." On other occasions—most notably an interview with Keiger, whose splendid profile was published in the alumni magazine of Tagg's alma mater, Penn State University—he'd said,

> Ninety percent of this business is disappointment. Anybody who trains horses is a pessimist, whether they admit it or not. If you're doing really, really, really well, you still

lose eighty percent of the time. And there's just so much that goes wrong. Every day you come to work there's usually something wrong. People say, "Aren't you excited?" But you can't get excited. The disappointments are just overwhelming.

One man's mood, however, was not about to spoil the party—at least not the Funny Cide party at Saratoga. Were you so inclined, you could now put Funny Cide hot sauce on your Funny Cide ice cream, and wash it down with Funny Cide beer or wine, while listening to the Funny Cide song on the Funny Cide CD. It seemed only a matter of time before Funny Cide droppings would be sold by the pound.

What did dampen opening-day spirits—and what flooded streets and soaked clothing and turned the main track to mud and forced the four races scheduled for the grass course to be shifted to the main track and caused thirty-seven horses to be scratched from the ten-race card and brought about the first opening day in eight years on which an attendance record was not set—was rain. And more rain. And still more.

The rain fell in torrents, through the morning, the afternoon, and all night. It was whatever you wanted to call it: cloudburst, deluge, downpour, and a dozen similar words that can be found in any thesaurus. It rained as if Saratoga was Louisiana, or Hawaii, or Southeast Asia. It rained so hard you couldn't see. And then it rained more. The word *monsoon* was spoken more frequently than *trifecta* at Saratoga on opening day, 2003.

Saratoga in the rain is not a destination resort. The stable areas are dismal, the training tracks treacherous, and the spectator areas at the racecourse itself, from the choicest box seats to the farthest reaches of the grandstand, are airless and dreary. Saratoga is meant to be a lawn party. In the rain, it has all the charm of a high school graduation ceremony that bad weather has forced into the gym.

Certainly, it was not a start to the meet that P. G. Johnson would want to remember. He ran a 40-1 shot in the first race, which, except for being the first race on opening day, was an inconsequential event. The horse finished ninth in a ten-horse field.

P.G. I wanted to be a horse trainer but I didn't know anything about horses. I'd almost never even seen a live horse. They had a few pulling milk wagons, but how the hell do you learn about horses in Chicago? What I did was I got myself a job at a riding academy, the Midway Riding Academy, which was nowhere near where I lived. I had to take the elevated way the hell out to Sixty-third Street and Cottage Grove Avenue, and then walk three blocks.

The old guy I worked with there—this would've been February of '41—he says, "Hey, Johnson, you want to fuck around with racehorses, you should go to the sale at the stockyard next Tuesday. They got a Thoroughbred in there this time." The Union Stockyards had a horse sale the first Tuesday of every month, but a Thoroughbred was unusual, because they sold mostly quarter horses in from the plains, where they'd been used to herd cattle.

Two days before the sale, there was a fire in the stockyard. It was the middle of winter, so they turned all the horses out on Halsted Avenue. It was icy, and the poor Thoroughbred slid on the ice and fell down and hurt his shoulder, besides which he might have inhaled some smoke. I saw him the day before the sale, and he was a sorry-looking son of a bitch. I had seventy-five dollars saved, but I had to work that night, so I gave the money to the old guy, and I told him to try to buy the horse. I didn't trust him for two minutes, but I had no choice.

The next day, the guy had the horse at the riding academy. I said, "How much did he cost?" He said, "Seventy-five dollars." I know he's a lying bastard—he probably didn't pay more than twenty-five—but I couldn't do anything about it. Besides, I was so excited. I was seventeen, still a punk, but now I've got a racehorse to train, and it's my own.

His name was Song Master, and they had written his breeding down on a paper. Because he came out of Canada, he'd never run, but he had been—and this is a matter of record—the third-highest-priced yearling at the Saratoga sale in 1939. He'd sold for seventy-five hundred dollars, and you could look that up. Now, I didn't know that when I bought him. All I knew was he might've got smoke and he fell on his shoulder, but I didn't care: He was a Thoroughbred.

After I got him, I dropped out of school so I could get on the racetrack. I wound up going to night school at the YMCA on Randolph Street—high school equivalency or whatever the hell they called it. I didn't want to go, but my father already was mad as hell I'd bought a racehorse, so I didn't have a choice about that, either.

I got a stall at the old Lincoln Fields, out in Crete. Way out past Chicago Heights, on the Route 1: Go, go, go, go, and you get to Crete. It's way out south. It's where Alsab won the Joliet Stakes. Old Goggles McCoy rode him; he's the one that invented the goggles that jockeys wear. Churchill Downs owned the track; they bought it from the Peabody Coal Company. Whirlaway, some great horses raced there. But it was out in the middle, even past Crete. The Trailways bus would stop and let you off. They weren't supposed to, but they did. The drivers were nice to me, probably because I was just a kid who owned a racehorse.

I'd get out there in the middle of the night, after night school, and I'd go into the tack room. There was a big black guy I shared it with. He taught me about living under those conditions: like make sure you have breakfast real early at the track kitchen, because the other cook who came on later was a dishwasher.

I rode Song Master every day. He was not a nice horse. His biggest habit was he'd prop—stop on a dime. And you'd keep going. They told me that he must've been an old battery horse. One old-timer told me, "You'd better use a battery on him, 'cause they must've done that with him to get him going." I wasn't going to fucking touch a battery—I'd have electrocuted myself. Not to mention I could've got ruled off, and I wasn't even on yet. Then the guy stabled next to me said, "Go buy some BBs and put 'em in an aspirin tin, and shake the BBs in his ear. He'll go." And he did.

Then they started racing up at Hawthorne and Sportsman's. Those were the two tracks right next to each other, on Cicero Avenue and Fifty-second Street. I was too young to get my trainer's license. You had to be twenty-one in Illinois. This old-timer, name of Gus Wolfson, for some reason—I'll never know why—he befriended me. He had a license, so we listed him as trainer, and we ran the horse a couple of times.

He didn't get anything at Hawthorne, so I took him to Beulah Park, in Grove City, Ohio. Anybody could get a license in Ohio. Charlie the Chinaman could get a license in Ohio. I ran Song Master two or three times. He was third, he was fourth, maybe second once, which wasn't so bad considering I had absolutely no background as a trainer. Poor goddamned horse: from Saratoga to Beulah Park by way of Canada and a fire in the Chicago stockyard, and he winds up with a teenage punk who had no idea of how the hell to train a racehorse.

How I learned was from older trainers, the way every kid does who pays attention. They treated me well because they figured I was too dumb to ever be a threat. But I got homesick as hell for Chicago. Problem was, you couldn't leave the Beulah Park grounds without a certificate from the feed man and the tack man that you'd paid your bills. And I hadn't. I couldn't. I had no money. You get forty dollars for second or third, and I ate—I was a good eater—and I was buying dinner for my exercise rider and his wife, and I paid the lady who owned the rooming house, and that was that.

Eventually, a van driver from Chicago recognized me. He must have felt sorry for me, because he got me and the horse out of there in the middle of the night. I went back to Hawthorne. I got a stall right away, and I run the horse in Gus's name, and he wins. But I still didn't have an Illinois license.

If you look at the record, Gus Wolfson's name is down as trainer, but I didn't want anybody to think I wasn't the trainer, so I got my own picture taken in the winner's circle. If you ever see the picture, the skinny kid in the leather jacket, with a fedora on, that was me. That was my maiden.

Right away, I wanted to hustle, I wanted to get more horses to train. So I went to Bill Hamilton, the steward, tough son of a bitch. He was the official starter for the Kentucky Derby for thirty years; then he became the state steward in Illinois, strictly a political job. He let every gangster that ever walked the earth be owners and trainers.

I went to him, and he said, "You're too young." So I showed him my license from Ohio. He said, "Well, by all rights I shouldn't do it, but you're not gonna go away, are you, boy?" I said, "No, sir." So he gave me the license. And that was my start.

6 Unless he's employed there, a man can do no good in the stable area of a racetrack before sunrise. The movement, in cramped quarters and in a compressed time frame, of dozens of high-strung, competitive, and potentially dangerous animals, each of which weighs more than a thousand pounds, creates considerable tension. Chitchat, even among the people involved in their care, is not encouraged. Less welcome is a visit from an outsider.

P.G. was gracious enough to point this out only obliquely, usually by shuffling to the end of the shed row farthest from me, while his assistant, Heriberto "Ocala" Cedano, a burly native of the Dominican Republic who had been with him for more than thirty years, glared at me as if I'd just made a pass at his wife.

After the first few mornings—once the fog of my thirty-year absence had burned off—I stopped showing up in the dark, and found that P.G. was much more affable in the light of day. This was not a matter of metabolism, but had to do with the structure of a trainer's working hours.

It's not that trainers especially like keeping the hours of a morning talk-show host or a dairy farmer, nor that the horses crave early-morning workouts. And while it's true that in more roguish times a slick trainer might have chosen to breeze an especially fast horse before dawn, figuring that the fewer people who knew how fast he really was, the more likely he'd be to go off at decent odds (a practice that gave rise to the term *dark horse*), the more prosaic reason for exercising horses early in the morning is that at many Thoroughbred facilities the same track used for training is also used for racing in the afternoon. The morning workouts tear up the surface, and several hours of maintenance are required for repair.

Thus, the first few hours at a barn are the busiest. The horses are led from their stalls, walked, taken to the track for the morning's run, led back, hosed and washed, walked again, put back in their stalls, and fed. Most of the day's work is done before many people who will go to the races in the afternoon have had breakfast.

P.G.'s barn was located at the northeastern end of the Oklahoma training track. The automobile and—new since my last visit, but now buzzing about as thick as mosquitoes—the golf cart had contracted the Saratoga backstretch considerably, but P.G. was still as far from the center of the morning action as a trainer could be, which was the way he wanted it. Like his friends Allen Jerkens and Barclay Tagg, he'd never seen a horse improved by being gawked at by strangers, and anyone he might need to talk to knew where to find him.

P.G. was far from antisocial, but after sixty years in the game, he'd become expert at avoiding those who annoyed him, or who displayed a propensity for wasting his time. Having sensed that he was the Saratoga personage whose professional life I most wanted to observe throughout the meeting, I put considerable effort into trying to stay out of either category.

Actually, if I hadn't considered him quite such a legend, and if his company had proved any less enjoyable, I might have spent my mornings elsewhere. When I was with him at the barn, even if I didn't ask questions, he tended to explain things to me. This required him to use his voice, which seemed in imminent danger of grinding to a permanent halt. I felt like apologizing every time I asked him a question that he could not answer with a nod or a shake of his head.

"It sounds as if it must hurt to talk," I finally said.

"Hell, no. It only hurts to listen."

He said he'd begun to grow hoarse about five years earlier, and that the condition had worsened steadily. Not only had no treatment proved effective, doctors hadn't yet agreed on a diagnosis.

"The new theory is that it must be environmental, some kind of allergy to stuff floating in the air around the barn. I don't know. If I was allergic to horseshit, I would've gone mute a hell of a long time ago. Which I know certain people around here wish I had."

"Why?"

He paused to adjust his toothpick. He'd given up cigars fifteen years earlier, when his granddaughter, Emma, was born, and his daughter wouldn't let him anywhere near her with a cigar. He started to chew toothpicks instead.

"Come here," he said, standing. "I'll show you why." We walked along the shed row. He stopped at a stall halfway down.

"This is a filly called Micmaceuse. Do you know what that word means?"

"No."

"Why the hell not? You're supposed to be an educated man, aren't you? Don't you speak French?"

"No, but I've got a daughter living in Paris."

"Don't matter. I'm not asking her."

"What does it mean?"

"It means 'troublemaker.' Now, go ask *my* daughter: not Karen from the *Racing Form;* Kathy, my older one, Emma's mother. She's the one who named it. She'll tell you: She named it after me. Because that's the reputation I've got."

"How come?"

"I've got a bad habit of saying whatever the hell I think,

and that's not something most guys around here will do. Take my friend, Allen Jerkens. He's smarter than me in a lot of respects, and he's been around New York even longer than me. This place could be blowing up, they could be robbing the trainers and the owners and the customers, and selling the horses for dog meat, and he'd find a way to talk his way around all that without saying anything against the house. Now, he won't go over there and sit with the big shots—he wouldn't do that—but you'd never get Allen to say shit if he had a mouthful of it."

He turned suddenly toward a groom whom I had not even realized he'd been watching. "Hey!" he growled, as loudly as he could, which wasn't very, "how long are you planning to leave that water bucket empty? That's no goddamn camel you got there, that's a horse."

———

The rain continued. It rained every day, it rained overnight, and it rained again the next morning. P.G. ran a horse in a $50,000 claiming race. The horse was owned by the wife of one of the biggest car dealers in New Jersey. It went off at 30-1, and finished next to last in a nine-horse field.

He ran another of the car dealer's wife's horses in an allowance race. This one went off at 16-1 and finished seventh.

"I got twenty-eight horses with me up here," P.G. said, "and except for Volponi and a four-year-old filly named She's Got the Beat, I'm not sure there's a one of them that's worth two dead flies."

Volponi was being pointed for the $750,000 Whitney Stakes, to be run on August 2. "I've never won the Whitney and I'd like to," P.G. said. "I like winning races named for rich guys."

He started She's Got the Beat in the $250,000 Go for Wand Handicap, which was run on the first Sunday of the meet, July 27. The biggest crowd of the season, more than 57,000, showed up. Most were less interested in the race than in the day's giveaway: a ceramic mug in a shape apparently meant to approximate Seabiscuit's head.

Like most of the horses in P.G.'s barn that he didn't own either outright or in partnership, She's Got the Beat belonged to the wife of the car dealer from New Jersey. Bettors were not impressed by the filly's resume. She was made fourth choice in the field of six, at odds of 20-1. The overwhelming favorite was Sightseek, widely considered the best female horse in the East, if not the country.

Sightseek was trained by Bobby Frankel. That alone would have been enough to send the horse off at 1-5. Through the spring and summer, Frankel not only had a horse in virtually every stakes race in New York, but won most of them.

As Saratoga opened in 2003, the *Daily Racing Form* commented that Frankel presided over "the most powerful barn in the history of American stakes racing." He'd become the emperor of what the *Racing Form* called the sport's "brave new world." He was paramount among the new breed of "super-trainers [who] achieve winning percentages that defy all the traditional norms of their profession."

That was as close as the *Racing Form*, which serves essentially as a house organ for the industry, would ever come to hinting that recurrent rumors about illegal stimulants still plagued Frankel, even after his ascendancy to the top of his profession. The difference from what I'd heard thirty years earlier was that the rumors now swirled about a much higher class of horse.

In the late 1980s, Frankel had begun training for the hugely wealthy California tuna magnate, Edmund "Chicken of the Sea" Gann. A few years later, he'd been chosen—by computer search, it was said (and this was widely believed, because only a computer would not have detected Frankel's caustic personality)—to train the horses raced in California (and at Saratoga) for Juddmonte Farms, the multinational racing empire presided over by a Saudi Arabian prince named Khalid Abdullah. As a result, the former in-your-face claiming trainer Bobby Frankel was having delivered to his doorstep dozens of the sort of championship-caliber horses that had eluded P.G. all his life.

Sightseek was a good example. Bred on Juddmonte's Kentucky farm, she had won six of ten lifetime starts, including two consecutive Grade I races in 2003. (Stakes races are classified annually as Grade I, Grade II, or Grade III, according to the amount of the purse, the quality of the entrants, and the traditional importance of the event.)

She's Got the Beat, while a talented and plucky filly, had never won any sort of stakes race. P.G. had trained her to her highest possible level, but neither on the basis of pedigree nor performance could she be considered comparable to Sightseek.

As it happened, none of the other starters was a match for Sightseek, either. Ridden by Jerry Bailey, the forty-five-year-old jockey who'd won the Eclipse Award as the best in America for the past three years, Frankel's filly cruised to the lead at the top of the stretch and romped by more than ten lengths. She's Got the Beat was second by five, a significantly better finish than the 20-1 odds had predicted.

From P.G.'s perspective, it was a satisfactory outcome, and it earned $50,000 in purse money for the car dealer's wife, but it underscored the difference between Bobby Frankel and himself: Frankel got his horses from Saudi Arabian princes and Southern California billionaires. P.G. got his—except for those he'd bred himself, such as Volponi—from the wife of a car dealer in New Jersey.

———

"I need some new blood," he said, later that day, back at his barn. "And I'm not talking about a transfusion. My problem is, a lot of my owners have died off or got out of the game in the past ten years, and the new ones don't even look in my direction. If I was a Supreme Court justice or a symphony conductor, they'd say I was experienced. In this game, they just call me old. And it don't help that I sound like gears grinding when I talk."

It was not as if P.G. was slowing down at seventy-seven. He got up at 2:30 A.M. every day. He drank a cup of coffee, then walked on his treadmill for half an hour. He either watched the 3 A.M. CNN rebroadcast of the previous night's Larry King show, or he studied pedigree charts while on the treadmill, depending on who was Larry King's guest. He arrived at his barn at 4:30 A.M., not only at Saratoga in the summer, but at Belmont Park during the coldest days of the New York winter.

"The horses don't know there's snow on the roads," he said. "It ain't like school, where they can call it off for bad weather. They'll cancel the racing in the afternoon, but you still got to take care of the horses in the morning." And this was seven days a week, with perhaps a week off for vacation every three or four years, and P.G. had been doing it for sixty years.

"Maybe you should take a little time away from the barn," I said one morning.

"What are you talking about?" he rasped. It was as if I'd said maybe he should become a vegetarian.

"For your voice. You know, if it's stuff in the air around here, maybe you should give yourself a break, go breathe clean air somewhere, see if that hoarseness goes away."

"Are you sneaking up on the word *retire?*"

"No, but—"

"Christ, you sound like my wife! Retire. Then what the hell do I do, sit home all day and watch television?"

"You could read books."

"I already read books. I'm reading one right now called *Charlie Wilson's War.* It's about the CIA in Afghanistan. Have you read it?"

"No."

"Why the hell not? I thought writers were supposed to read books. Listen, I'm not going to retire. It took me sixty years to get a big horse. Why the hell should I walk away now?"

"For your health?"

"You just met me and already you're trying to get me out of the game? Now, I'm definitely not going to introduce you to my wife. All I need is that retirement crap from two sides. I say to Mary Kay all the time: 'You want to keep me alive a little longer? You still want to see a smile on my face once in a while? Then just let me be with my horses.' A trainer is all I ever wanted to be since I was sixteen years old, and I think if you can do exactly what you want in life for sixty years, you're one lucky son of a bitch.

"All I need—I don't actually need 'em, but I'd sure like to have 'em—is a couple of new owners with enough money not to worry about it for a while, and enough sense not to try to tell me what to do. Then I could take the horses to Florida for the winter—I haven't wintered down there for ten years—and I'd sit in the sun and get my voice back and bring along the new two-year-olds nice and slow, and have a few good meals with Allen Jerkens and Barclay, and I'd come back to New York in the spring and show a few people that I still got some surprises up my sleeve." He smiled and turned his face to the morning sun, which was making a rare appearance. It was 10 A.M., almost time for his lunch.

P.G. I wound up in the Merchant Marine in the war, back and forth to Liverpool on the Liberty ships. When I got out, I claimed a horse at Fairmount—that's in Collinsville, Illinois, down by St. Louis— for fifteen hundred dollars. A nice horse, named Dridas.

The thing about him was, you'd work him and he'd cool out all right, but the next morning he'd be dead spanking lame. One of the guys from Fairmount told me, "Hey, boy, don't worry about it, you're all right. When that horse was a yearling he ran through a fence, and he got a bunch of splinters up into his shoulder, and they got them all out, but one was too close to the main artery, and they didn't touch it. You just got to walk him a lot, warm him up real good; he'll be fine." You see, there wasn't a lot of surgery on horses in those days. There was more autopsies than surgeries.

So I took him to Florida for the winter and turned him out on a farm. I brought him up to Hawthorne when racing started again in Chicago after the war. They ran the Lincoln Fields meeting at Hawthorne because of the gas shortage. But I'll tell you, that farmer in Florida must have been having a feed shortage, because when Dridas came back he looked like woe-is-begone. He was skinny to begin with, and now he looked like somebody had reached in and pulled his guts out. But what could I do? I only had two horses, and the other, she was absolutely no-account.

I work Dridas one day, and he worked pretty good, and the next morning, of course, he was lame. Now, the guy in the stable next to me was a vet, Doc Boyens, and to this day I always say no veterinarian can train a horse. Doc Boyens says, "Your horse worked pretty good the other day, but he's lame. Can I help you?" This, now, was innocent. I said, "No, he's okay; he'll be fine." And like a sap I told him the story.

Opening day, I put him in—a twenty-five-hundred-dollar claimer. He wins. After the race, they say, "Take him back to the paddock, he's claimed." "Oh, shit, who claimed him?" "Doc Boyens." "*Doc Boyens?*"

He comes over. "Let me explain—"

Wham! I hit him here, I hit him here, I knocked him down. And the next thing I know they're pulling me off him. He was about thirty-five years old, maybe forty, not too old to hit. Tell you the truth, after he did that to me, if he'd have been ninety I'd have hit him. Later, I looked at the claim slip: "Don Ameche." Son of a bitch almost put me out of business so he could claim my horse for Don Ameche, the movie actor.

Cost me a hundred-dollar fine, which was a lot of money

in those days, but it was worth it. The reason I hit him wasn't because he made the claim—though that was dirty, claiming one of only two horses a new kid had—but because he'd come by my barn as a vet, like he was trying to help me out. In fact, he'd told me I should enter the horse in that claiming race; it would help him get over his lameness. First and last time I ever punched a man on the racetrack. What I learned was the golden rule of the claiming game: Do unto others before they do unto you.

ANNE M. EBERHARCT

P. G. Johnson

7   **I made it a point to spend as much time as possible watching Volponi. He was not a cozy horse to be around. He was very big and much more heavily muscled than the** other horses in P.G.'s barn. He was not vicious or mean-spirited, but he was tough and he knew it. He was a horse that seemed quite aware of his stature, not only physically, but in terms of accomplishment. He seemed to know he was enti-tled to respect.

The competitive instinct that had enabled him to win the Breeders' Cup Classic was not something that could be switched on and off, as everyone who worked with him in P.G.'s barn had learned, some more easily than others. He was not an animal to trifle with, or to take for granted.

Volponi had a younger half brother named Gentle Nudge (same dam, different sire) on the premises with him, but the two horses could not have been more different in either performance or demeanor.

Gentle Nudge—named by P.G. after considerable thought as to what a pleasant tap on prom night might be called (Pleasant Tap being the sire, Prom Knight the dam)—was a three-year-old who'd run third in his first start, but who had gotten progressively worse after that. In his three most recent races, he had not finished better than eighth.

But he was not only gentle, he was genial, and unlike Volponi, who knew Saratoga was only the next arena in which high performance would be expected of him, Gentle Nudge seemed to view it as the ideal place for a summer vacation.

Another difference—and not a small one—between P.G.'s big horse and the big horse's little half brother was that while Gentle Nudge had not yet demonstrated that he was worth the price of a tub of oats, Volponi had been privately valued at $10 million over the winter.

What's more, intending to retire the horse at the end of the 2003 season, P.G. was actively trying to sell him.

"I got a lot of people interested," he said. "There's two groups from Japan that'll be looking at him up here; there's Brereton Jones, he used to be governor of Kentucky; there's Mr. Farish, he's the ambassador to England right now, but he's got a hell of a stud farm in Kentucky; there's Stronach, that Austrian from Canada whose Magna group is buying up half the racetracks in America, and there's a lot of other people."

"How much do you think you'll get for him?" I asked.

"I don't know. Ask me again after he wins the Whitney next week."

———

Of all P.G.'s horses, only Volponi had won any sort of stakes race in 2002. Of the country's top fifty trainers, as ranked by the *Thoroughbred Times*, P.G.—forty-second on the list— had been the only one with just a single stakes winner in his barn.

Were one to have put it crudely, if not entirely accurately, one might have said that P.G. had one big horse and a bunch of dogs. And not even Volponi had yet won in 2003.

He'd started three times, finishing second in each race. He'd been beaten by a neck in a seven-furlong allowance at Belmont in May, he'd run second in the Grade II Brooklyn Handicap at Belmont in mid-June, and then had run his best race of the year in the Grade I Suburban at Belmont over the July 4th weekend.

In that race, however, the four-year-old Mineshaft,

owned by William Farish, the ambassador, had run the race of his life and had beaten Volponi by two lengths. Mineshaft had come to Saratoga, but only to rest for his fall campaign.

In the Whitney, Volponi's chief rival looked to be Medaglia d'Oro, the Bobby Frankel four-year-old that Volponi had beaten in the Classic the previous fall. Having won his only two starts of the year—Grade II stakes at Santa Anita and at Oaklawn Park—Medaglia d'Oro probably would be favored over Volponi in the Whitney.

This irked P.G. He felt that his horse had never received the credit he deserved. Because he'd been a 43-1 shot, Volponi's win had been considered a fluke. And because his win exposed the biggest attempted wagering scam in racing history, most of the stories in the aftermath were about the failed betting coup, not the winner.

Three former fraternity brothers from Drexel University in Philadelphia, one of whom worked as a programmer at Autotote, a company that processed off-track bets, had devised a fraudulent method for winning racing's most exotic wager, the Pick Six. They employed it on Breeders' Cup Day, but because the long shot Volponi won the last of the races involved, there were only six winning tickets in the country, each worth more than $500,000.

Curiously enough, all six had been sold to the same person. Curiously enough, all six reflected the peculiar pattern of selecting only one horse in each of the first four Pick Six races, then all the horses in the last two.

Red lights flashed and sirens wailed. Investigation unearthed the illegal tinkering with the Autotote data that had enabled the three ex–frat brothers, in essence, to make their bets after the first four races had already been run. The money was never paid, and all three scammers went to prison. Volponi became known as "FBI Horse of the Year," and started being referred to as "Special Agent Volponi," which everybody but P.G. found amusing.

———

During the waterlogged mornings leading up to the Whitney on August 2, more and more reporters began to show up at P.G.'s barn. The local press—and another difference between 2003 and 1971 was that there was little evidence of any other kind at Saratoga—had begun to treat the Volponi–Medaglia d'Oro rematch as an event second in importance only to the looming Funny Cide–Empire Maker battle in the Travers.

But P.G. wouldn't follow the script. "Frankel's horse doesn't worry me," he said. "He's just getting all the hype." He knew, of course, that any reporter to whom he said this would immediately go to Bobby Frankel's barn for a reaction, and he knew that Frankel would be upset. In P.G.'s view, any course of action that succeeded in upsetting Bobby Frankel was worth pursuing.

There were specific personal reasons for P.G.'s antipathy toward Frankel, but mostly, it seemed, he was annoyed by what he considered Frankel's arrogance.

In any event, he kept insisting that Volponi had nothing to fear from Medaglia d'Oro, and that he had nothing to fear from Bobby Frankel. "When you run against Mr. Frankel, are you running against his horse or his ego?" he said. Within half an hour one could almost see the steam rising from the roof of Frankel's barn.

Then P.G. went further, saying, "When I worry, I worry more about Puzzlement, because I worry more about Jerkens than I do Frankel." To me, he was even more direct. "You know the difference between Jerkens and Frankel?" he said. "Jerkens trains with his brain, not his mouth."

I remembered Allen Jerkens. Even in 1971, he was something of a legend in New York racing. A native of Long Island, a ferocious polo player, and the son of an Austrian cavalry officer, he won his first race at the old Aqueduct in 1950, when he was only twenty years old. He was New York's leading trainer four times in the 1950s and 1960s, winning his first title at age twenty-seven. Training for Jack Dreyfus, founder of the Dreyfus Fund, Jerkens had beaten the fabled Kelso three times in 1962 with a horse called Beau Purple.

In 1973, Jerkens beat Secretariat twice in consecutive

races, with different horses, and became known forever after as the Giant Killer. In 1975, at forty-five, he became the youngest trainer ever elected to the Hall of Fame. Renowned almost as much for his reticence as for his horsemanship, he gave the shortest acceptance speech on record: "Hello. Thank you. Good-bye."

At seventy-four, after almost dying of pancreatitis in Florida early in 2002, he'd come back to Saratoga with some of the most talented horses he'd had in years. Though still far from gregarious, Jerkens had developed a sort of benign avuncularity as he aged.

Though he abhorred formality, Jerkens was again spending so much time in the winner's circle that he'd taken to wearing a seersucker sports jacket and wide necktie to the races in the afternoon. He'd also taken to wearing a wide-brimmed hat that, in combination with his large physical stature, made him look like a candidate for, say, governor of Georgia, circa 1940.

Jerkens and P.G. had been almost like brothers for decades. Both were friendly with Barclay Tagg. I came to consider the three of them the Three Wise Men of Saratoga, and—because Tagg was more or less quarantined with Funny Cide Fever—when I wasn't with P.G. in the mornings, I gravitated toward Jerkens, who displayed an unfailing courtesy that belied his curmudgeonly reputation.

Despite the Giant Killer's history of overachievement,

P.G.'s pronouncements that Jerkens's horse was a greater threat to Volponi than was Frankel's seemed more mischievous than heartfelt. Puzzlement was a four-year-old of modest accomplishment. He'd won an allowance race at the Whitney distance of a mile and an eighth on the second day of the Saratoga meeting, but had never finished in the money in a stakes.

And Jerkens himself was making no claims on behalf of his horse. Jerkens, in fact, was making no claims of any sort. He trained his horses in the morning, and when not at the races in the afternoon, he dug for dandelion roots behind his barn. He was a great believer in feeding dandelion roots to his horses. He also was a great believer in saying nothing of interest—or, better yet, nothing at all—to the press.

———

"Dad, why can't you be more like Allen Jerkens?" P.G.'s daughter Karen asked one morning. Her *Daily Racing Form* job required her to speak to Bobby Frankel almost daily.

"You want me to change my personality just so Frankel will keep talking to you?"

"No, he'll talk to me no matter what, but—"

"Of course, he will. He can't shut up."

"Well, you're not exactly setting a good example."

"Pay attention," P.G. said to me. "This is the first time in history a reporter ever told a guy he talked too much."

"I'm speaking as your daughter," she said. "I don't want to see you embarrass yourself."

"I've been doing it for fifty years. Why stop now?"

"Maybe because it's also embarrassing me?"

"Don't worry. The way my voice is going, I'll be using sign language by the end of the meeting. Then even Frankel will feel sorry for me."

"I doubt that," Karen said. "Right now, he's saying he'd like to come over here and kick your ass."

"An old man like him? Let him try. Over Ocala's dead body he'll kick my ass."

P.G. Let me tell you about my first great benefactor, Gus Wolfson. The one thing I didn't understand—besides why the hell he was so nice to me—was how he had any money. He didn't have a job, and he wasn't any kind of gambler, either. After a couple of years, I found out.

I'd been down south. You know the circuit: Hawthorne, Sportsman's, Detroit Fair Grounds—I couldn't race at Arlington in those days because my horses weren't good enough—and then for the fall you go to Keeneland and Churchill, and then New Orleans and Hot Springs for the winter, and back up through Kentucky in the spring. Everybody did that. We were like a traveling circus, except we were always trying to cut each other's balls off for a dollar.

Anyway, I get back to Chicago one year and I'm asking, "Where's old Gus?" They said, "You mean the graveyard robber? He's gone for good."

Now, I forget what the hell prison they had him in, but what he'd been doing (and apparently he'd been doing it for years) was he'd read in the papers about any rich Jew who died in Chicago. He'd find out where the burial was going to be and he'd get out there, all dressed up in a black suit and shiny black shoes, and he'd pretend to be some kind of official at the cemetery, and he'd help all the mourners out of their cars. Then, when he got them up to the grave site and the service started, he'd go back through the cars and steal the money out of the handbags. Son of a bitch got away with it for years. I never did see him again, but I'll never forget him for how much he helped me at the start.

Don't forget, this was Chicago in the forties, and there were some people around the racetrack in those days who hadn't turned out exactly the way their mothers wanted. And starting out I'd train for anybody. I didn't care, as long as they didn't try to tell me what to do.

There was one time I was going along with six or seven horses and doing pretty good, and Judge Hamilton, the steward who gave me my license, sends for me.

"Sit down." He didn't waste words. Sitting next to him was Clyde Trout, a good trainer, trained for Ada Rice, bigtime. Judge Hamilton says, "Clyde's got two horses that he can't train anymore, because he's got a contract now with Mr. Rice. And the owners need a trainer and they came to me, and I recommended you." One of the horses was named Thumbed Man, he was a pretty good horse, and the other one I don't remember. So I said, "Fine. Who's the owner?" But

Clyde just said, "I'll bring the horses over to your barn tomorrow."

He did, and not long afterwards this guy comes by, all dressed up, said his name was Dominic Di Bella. He says, "The horses run in my wife's name. We'll pay you in cash; don't worry about it." So I trained 'em. Never had any trouble, everything was good, and one day another trainer says, "You know who you're training for, don't you?"

I said, "Mr. Di Bella and his wife. I don't really know them, but he's a nice guy."

"You're not training for him," the guy tells me. "You're training for Golfbag Sam Hunt."

I said, "Oh, Jesus! You've got to be kidding me."

But he wasn't. Golfbag Sam Hunt was the biggest collector in Chicago for the loan sharks and the bookmakers. He was right down there with the worst: Anthony Accardo, Willie Bioff, "Cherry Nose" Gioe, Murray "The Camel" Humphreys, Frank Nitti, John Roselli. And one of his girlfriends was Norma Wallace, who ran all the best whorehouses in New Orleans.

He started coming out to the barn on Sunday mornings with Di Bella. Never said much, just "When's he gonna run?" So, I'd tell him. That was all. Just like any other guy who owned horses.

But I remember one Sunday morning—this was at

Sportsman's, out in Cicero—he left to go back downtown. Now, before you got to the outer drive, you went through an area called Washington Park, which had turned into a black neighborhood, but with beautiful stone houses from the old days. There wasn't too many poor black people living there.

Anyway, he's heading downtown with his bodyguard, and he has a little fender bender. There's all these people with their finery (you know how black people dress for church: kids with pink dresses and so on), and he got out, and this black guy was mad, he'd bumped his LaSalle or whatever it was, and he's cursing at Sam Hunt and Sam reaches into his pocket and takes out enough money to choke two horses and says, "Here. I don't think it'll cost anything, but take it, I'm sorry." He apologized to the guy.

"You white motherfucker! You can't come through here driving like that in our neighborhood!" And on like that. Now, this is as the story goes; I wasn't there myself to see it. Al reaches back in his golf bag and pulls out this little snub-nosed machine gun, which is why he carried the golf bag—he never played golf in his life—and he killed the guy and a couple of other people, too. Puts the gun back in the bag, and by the time he gets downtown the whole Chicago Police Department is waiting.

"Sam, what happened?" "The niggers tried to kill me. I bumped one of their cars, and I took money out of my pocket to settle it, and they robbed the money and started to pound on my car. I was lucky to get away alive." And that was the end of it. The cops weren't going to make trouble for Sam Hunt just because he killed a couple of black guys. That's how Chicago was in those days.

Volponi and groom

JOSEPH DIORIO/HORSEPHOTOS

8 Volponi's jockey, Jose Santos, was a forty-two-year-old Chilean with strong hands and a quick smile. In the late 1980s, he was the leading rider in New York and the leading money winner among all jockeys in America. In 1987, he rode Volponi's sire, Cryptoclearance, to a fourth-place finish in the Kentucky Derby. But he broke his hip, arm, and collarbone in a spill at Belmont in 1992, and, between that and an unsettled personal life, it had taken him years to get back to the top.

By the summer of 2003, however, he was riding higher than ever. Not only had he won the Breeders' Cup Classic with Volponi, but in May he'd won his first Kentucky Derby, aboard Funny Cide.

Santos would ride Volponi in the Whitney. The next morning, he would head for New Jersey, where he'd be aboard Funny Cide in the $1 million Haskell Invitational at Monmouth Park. I had no idea how he'd handled his earlier success, but from everything I saw and heard at Saratoga, Santos was the personification of class this time around.

Indeed, while Medaglia d'Oro would no doubt be the betting favorite, the combination of P.G. and Santos made Volponi the overwhelming sentimental choice. As columnist Matt Graves wrote in the *Albany Times-Union,* "Most of today's trainers have too many horses to tend to and too little time to talk about them. Not Phil Johnson. You won't find a guy happier with his job anywhere in the world." The same could have been said of Santos, and Santos himself would have been the first to say it.

So much rain had fallen during the first ten days of the meet that 50 percent of the races scheduled for the grass had to be shifted to the main track.

So much rain had fallen that P.G. had bought waterproof baseball caps for Allen Jerkens, Barclay Tagg, and himself. "Barclay can't wear his," P.G. said. "It doesn't fit. His head is too pointy from all those horses he fell off when he used to be a jump rider."

So much rain had fallen that mushrooms were overrunning the grass on the tiny lawn in front of my cottage.

But the sun came out for the Whitney, and the track was fast. The race had drawn a field of seven and a crowd of 38,000, the largest of the meet except for a bobblehead souvenir day.

It was clear why Medaglia d'Oro was favored. After finishing out of the money in the 2002 Kentucky Derby and Preakness, he had run second in the Belmont Stakes and then had won the Travers. At Saratoga, people tended to remember the Travers. He'd also won his only two starts of 2003, and he would be ridden by Jerry Bailey. The only thing not to like, perhaps, was that he hadn't raced in four months. But, like P.G. himself, Bobby Frankel was known to be particularly adept at bringing a good horse back from a layoff.

Despite P.G.'s comments in the morning papers that Volponi was "better than he's ever been," and "I truly believe he is sitting on top of a big race," Medaglia d'Oro was 4-5 at post time. Volponi was second choice at 5-2. Despite P.G.'s high regard for Allen Jerkens, Puzzlement was 20-1.

———

No racehorse likes the starting gate, but most can be schooled to tolerate it, and many develop almost an indifference to it over time. Volponi was not one of these. He was not only big—seventeen hands, by racetrack measurement—but ungainly, and somewhat awkward. The more time I'd spent around him, the more I'd come to think that he had the personality of a heavyweight boxing champion: well-mannered and courteous as long as you didn't get in his face, but with an aura that suggested the potential for violence.

The starting gate got in Volponi's face.

In the Whitney, this was literally true.

Having drawn post position six, Volponi was led into the gate next to last. Shifting his weight from left to right and pawing the ground, he turned his head to the right when the number-seven horse moved in alongside him. Then, unease getting the better of him, he swung his neck sharply to the left. Just inside him, Medaglia d'Oro stood composed and focused.

The assistant starter assigned to Volponi reached for the horse's bridle in an attempt to straighten his head. At the same time, he shouted, "No, no, no!" to the starter, indicating that Volponi was not ready.

Apparently, the starter thought the assistant had shouted, "Go!" instead of "No!"

He pressed the button, the bell rang, the doors banged open, and the race began—with Volponi still standing flat-footed and looking sideways.

Knowing how much ground he'd lost before Volponi even got out of the gate, Santos rode him aggressively, if not quite frantically, from the start. He moved the horse up the outside, then cut to the inside, then seemed blocked behind horses and swung to the outside again.

In his box seat, P.G. muttered, "Jesus Christ, he's taking the scenic route."

Even so, once Volponi finally found running room in the homestretch it looked as if he might win the race. He drew to within half a length of Medaglia d'Oro at the eighth pole, but at that point what was being referred to as the "Frankel Factor" kicked in. Like so many of Frankel's other stakes horses, Medaglia d'Oro seemed to get a second wind an eighth of a mile from the finish, and Volponi, already used so hard after the unlucky start, was simply unable to catch him.

Medaglia d'Oro won by a length. Volponi was second by a length and a quarter. Puzzlement closed late to be fourth. Second place in the Whitney was worth $150,000, but one would not have guessed that from P.G.'s grim silence as he left the box. This loss had hurt more than most, not least because P.G. would be convinced for the rest of his life that he had had the better horse on the day.

———

In the winner's circle, Bobby Frankel was exultant. "I've got a good horse," he said. "Everybody knows he's a good horse except one guy who did not think he was a good horse and that guy finished second."

"Did what he said bother you?" somebody asked.

"Of course it bothered me. I wanted to kick his ass. But I learned a long time ago that the best revenge is winning. He's eating crow right now."

Actually, P.G. ate ground sirloin that night. But he was no happier on Sunday morning, having watched numerous video replays of the race.

"I fired him" was the first thing he said to me at the barn.

"You fired who?"

"That goddamned pinhead is who. How many lengths do you think he cost me?"

"The starter? How can you fire the starter?"

"Not that fucking horse whisperer. I mean that god-damned pinhead Santos."

"You fired Santos?"

"I sure as hell did. He's a goddamned bus driver. He should get a job with that company, the Gray Line Tours. He gave me the grand scenic tour of every inch of that race-track—inside, outside, up and down, and inside out. It's a miracle we finished as close as we did. My horse must've run a mile and a quarter instead of a mile and an eighth."

In the racing world, this was going to be big news. Santos was a member of the Funny Cide family, part of the feel-good story of the year. And no doubt he'd ride Funny Cide to yet another major victory in a million-dollar race that very day. There was no way that P.G. was going to come out of this looking like the grand old man of Saratoga. He already had Bobby Frankel crowing at him. The dismissal of Santos at the height of his popularity would make P.G. look querulous, and possibly foolish as well.

"What did he say?" I asked.

"He didn't say nothing because he doesn't know it yet. He didn't come back here last night, at least not while I was here, and he's down in New Jersey today. I'm trying to get hold of his agent right now. I'll tell him to his face tomorrow morning."

"You know, this may not go over so well. Like with the press."

"You think I give a damn about that? I give a damn about my horse. He's been second four times this year, beaten a total of six lengths. I think he finally deserves a decent ride. Santos has ridden him seven times, and he's only won with him once."

"But that was a big one."

"So was yesterday. Forty-plus years I've been up here and that's the first horse I ever ran in the Whitney."

"But firing Santos—everybody who loves Funny Cide will hate you."

"It's my horse, and it's my right to make a decision."

"Yeah, but Funny Cide is going to win that million-dollar race at Monmouth this afternoon, and they'll be building a statue of Santos on Broadway tomorrow morning."

"Don't be too sure," P.G. said. "This has always been a funny game."

P.G. with cigar

P.G.

The next spring—it would've been, I guess, '47, '48—we're at Keeneland, staying at the Campbell House in Lexington, and gettin' ready to ship to Churchill Downs. A guy calls me from the stable there and he says, "Phil, don't ship, you got no stalls here. I don't know what it is, but there's a sign at the gate not to let your van in."

So Mary Kay and I drive to Louisville the next morning. I go to the stall guy and he says, "Look, I don't know what this is all about, but I can't give you stalls." I said, "Where did this come from?" All he did was point up. I said, "From God?" He says, "Worse: from Sam McMcckin."

This McMeekin was the city manager of Louisville, and he was also the head steward at Churchill Downs. So I said, "Come on, Mary Kay, let's go see this guy." We go up to his office—we were dressed properly, ready for anything—and he says, "Come in, sit down. What's your problem?" I told him. He said, "What's your last name?" I said, "Johnson." He said, "Are you the Johnson from Chicago?" I said, "Yes."

Now, they had whitecaps called Andy Frayne ushers there, and he says to one, "Escort this couple off the grounds. We don't want any Chicago gangsters here." Just like that. We were gone.

Shit, we got big trouble now. Whatever's wrong, I'd better straighten it out. So I went back and I drove in through the stable gate again, and I go to Larry Thomson, who's a trainer, and the head of the Horsemen's Benevolent in Kentucky and Chicago. I told him the story. He said, "Have you done anything wrong?" I said, "No." "Have you got any rulings against you?" I told him about the time I popped Doc Boyens in the mouth, but this was long after that.

So he said, "All right, the Thoroughbred Racing Protective Bureau started last fall. They're going to be the police force for all the tracks, and they have an office here. I'll take you to the office so they don't throw you out again, and you can ask them about it." Now, Mary Kay is very upset. She's red in the face. She's almost crying. And we go in. They have no idea what's the problem.

Then it dawns on me. I said, "I think I know why," and I told them the whole story about Golfbag Sam. But I said, "I don't have any horses with them anymore." "Why don't you?" I said, "Because last fall when I was here we were staying at the Brown Hotel and one of those guys from that group called me to come down to the lobby, and he said, 'We're going to pick those two horses up today.' He told me about the new racing police coming in. He said, 'We're going to do our business a different way. And we want you to be clean.' Now, they didn't give a shit about me. This was because originally I had been recommended by Hamilton, and they didn't want any obvious links to him. So I said, 'Thank you,' and he says, 'We gave you a stopwatch to use. We want that back.' So I went upstairs. I said, 'Mary Kay, give me the stopwatch.' I took it down, and that was the end of it. We went to New Orleans."

I told them everything. They said, "But how did you get those horses to train in the first place?" Now, it's four or five o'clock in the afternoon, and other than going to the bathroom, we haven't had a drink of water all day. One guy's name was Vince Murphy and the other was Joe Kerjenic, a former North Chicago motorcycle cop. (I later rented a house with him on Lake Pontchartrain for the Fair Grounds meeting in New Orleans, and he was head of the TRPB at

Churchill Downs years later, when I brought in Naskra for the Derby.)

"How did you meet these people? If you don't tell us that, we can't help you." I said, "I was called to the steward's one day," and I told them the names of the horses so they would know Clyde Trout had been training the horses. And I said, "Clyde Trout was there, and the steward was there, and he recommended me to Clyde Trout." "Who was the steward?" I said, "Bill Hamilton." They told us to come back the next morning.

Next day, eleven o'clock, Kerjenic says, "Now I'm going to call Bill Hamilton while you're sitting there." Picked up the phone and got him and told him the story about me. And Hamilton said, "You dumb son of a bitches, that's the cleanest kid we ever had in Chicago. You get that fucking McMeekin on the telephone and I'll tell him." Remember, he started the Derby for thirty-three years, so he was a Kentuckian. He wasn't too clean, but he was a Kentuckian.

They said, "No, we don't need him to talk to you." See, they didn't want him cursing at McMeekin. So they called McMeekin, and they told him word for word, except for the swear words, what Bill Hamilton said. Then they told me, "Mr. McMeekin wants to see you upstairs. You're fine now, don't worry about it."

So we went upstairs, and everybody is eating lunch, because the races are starting. McMeekin shakes hands with us, and puts his arm around Mary Kay's shoulder. "Don't be upset. Sit down, I want you to have lunch with me." In the director's room at Churchill. And that was the end of it. I had my horses in the stalls the next day.

9 It seemed strange that Funny Cide, who had become essentially the patron saint of Saratoga, would race in New Jersey on August 3, while Empire Maker, trained by the Darth Vader of the saga, Bobby Frankel, would run at Saratoga the same day. But even if they were sentimental fools, Funny Cide's owners were no bumpkins when it came to cashing in.

The Haskell Invitational at Monmouth had a purse of $1 million, while the Jim Dandy at Saratoga the same day offered only half that. In addition, Funny Cide would not have to face Empire Maker in New Jersey. In the Triple Crown races, they'd beaten each other once (Empire Maker having skipped the Preakness), but most racing people considered Empire Maker to be the better horse, and there was a sense at Saratoga that the Funny Cide bunch did not want to risk spoiling their summer-long party by submitting to a rubber match before the Travers.

Their scenario went something like this: Empire Maker wins the Jim Dandy, while Funny Cide beats Frankel's second-best three-year-old, Peace Rules, at Monmouth. Then

Funny Cide comes "home"—admittedly to a track he's never raced on—for the $1 million Travers, which in the meantime could be hyped even more hysterically than it already has been. The brewery would have to run 24/7 to turn out enough Funny Cide Lite.

August 3 was one of the longest and most uncomfortable days of the entire Saratoga season. The temperature was in the upper 80s, as usual; the humidity was close to 100 percent, as usual; and a crowd of 65,000 swarmed the track for a T-shirt giveaway.

The Jim Dandy would not be run until almost 5:30 P.M., while the Haskell, to be televised live on screens throughout the Saratoga track, would start twenty minutes later.

Only five horses besides Empire Maker, the 3-10 favorite, had been entered in the Jim Dandy, and only one of them, Strong Hope—a $1.7 million yearling who'd won four consecutive races for Saratoga's leading trainer, Todd Pletcher—was seen as any sort of challenger. The race shaped up as another slam dunk for Bobby Frankel, and not much more than a diversion before the main event, which would be Funny Cide's triumph at Monmouth.

But who was it who said that racing was a funny game?

Not Bobby Frankel, who watched the Jim Dandy in the privacy of the racing secretary's office, and who later refused to say anything.

And not Jerry Bailey, who rode Empire Maker to a second-place finish, beaten a half-length by Strong Hope. "They're horses, they're not machines," Bailey said.

And not Barclay Tagg, from sweltering Monmouth, where the favored Funny Cide ran a dull and distant third, beaten nine lengths by Frankel's Peace Rules. "I wanted him laying third behind two horses," Tagg said. "Santos thought he ought to be laying behind four. I said, 'If that's the way you feel, you do that.' But when you take too much of a hold of this horse it discourages him."

And not Jose Santos, who said, "At one point, I thought he was going to be last," and who returned to Saratoga that night to learn that not only had he just lost a big race, he'd also lost a big horse—Volponi.

Not that it really mattered who said it. What mattered was that in less than half an hour, at the end of a suffocating Sunday afternoon, the upcoming Travers had gone from being potentially the biggest race in Saratoga history to a contest between two beaten favorites who would be trying to make amends.

———

Matters got decidedly unfunnier the next day.

Funny Cide came back from New Jersey with a fever: not

Funny Cide Fever, but a real one, as in a temperature of 102, which indicated infection to approximately the same extent as in a human.

Barclay Tagg had always known that something like this was going to happen. "You live with disappointment in this game," he said. "There are a lot more downs than ups."

Welcome, Sackatoga Stable, to the 90 percent.

"I'll live if I don't get him to the Travers," Tagg said, "and I'm not going to kill the horse trying to do it. I'm not going to be pressured. I was pressured into the Preakness and the Belmont; I'm not going to be pressured into anything else."

More rain fell. When it wasn't raining, the humidity was so awful you wished it was. Bobby Frankel went back to California to check on his horses at Del Mar, where the weather was glorious every day and the Pacific Ocean was only a long Frisbee toss from the track. It was clear that he didn't feel appreciated at Saratoga. "I know I'm making enemies right now," he said. "Owners and other trainers, a lot of them are jealous. I know how it is. No one is going to feel sorry for me if I lose. I won't get any sympathy."

More rain fell. Grass racing was only a memory. The Oklahoma track turned so soupy and slippery that many trainers, including P.G., simply stopped working their horses. "They hurt themselves easy enough on a good track," P.G. said. "I'm not going to send 'em out on a mess like that."

Funny Cide was on antibiotics, and his fever was coming down, but Barclay Tagg, needless to say, was not optimistic.

"Barclay's goin' mental," P.G. said. "It's just too much stress for him, all those reporters crowding around every day, wanting every goddamned blood test result. He ought to tell 'em if they want to know the horse's temperature they can stick the thermometer up his ass themselves."

A new owner sent Tagg a three-year-old filly from Delaware Park named Island Fashion. Tagg planned to run her in the Alabama Stakes the following weekend. "She's a pretty nice filly," he said. From him, this was extravagant praise. I made a note to bet her in the Alabama. Maybe I could win back what I'd lost on Volponi in the Whitney.

Jose Santos, naturally, wasn't pleased to have lost the mount on Volponi. "P.G. makes the boo-boo by shooting his mouth off at Frankel, then when he loses he takes it out on the little guy, me," he said.

In response, P.G. said, "I took him off because I think he gave the horse a terrible ride."

He then announced that Volponi would run next in the Saratoga Breeders' Cup Handicap on August 16, and that he would be ridden by the one jockey in the world who everyone would have to admit was an improvement over Santos: Jerry Bailey.

———

Mornings with P.G. were always educational.

I learned, for example, that the vaginas of fillies are sewn shut during their racing careers, in order to prevent irritation caused by dirt kicked up from the track.

I learned that male horses who demonstrated excessive libido had their nostrils smeared with Vicks VapoRub or an equivalent, so they wouldn't be aroused by the scent of a nearby female.

I learned that, in horses, at least, blackberries can cure diarrhea, and that the incidence of transvestism among grooms is much higher than in the general population. In neither case did I learn why.

Perhaps the most interesting thing I learned was that the Saudi Arabian prince who owned 2001 Kentucky Derby winner War Emblem had traveled not only with bodyguards, but with a "body parts" man, from whom a vital organ could be taken if the prince suddenly found himself in need of a replacement. Even that, however, hadn't prevented him from dying of a heart attack.

My afternoons were less educational. I only learned things that I already knew: that I was a mediocre handicapper and a dumb, impulsive bettor, and that enough heat and humidity could turn any carnival into an ordeal.

Evenings were varied. Were I younger, they would have been more so, I'm sure, with at least some ending among the rowdy crowd surrounding ex–steeplechase rider turned journalist Sean Clancy at the Parting Glass. (Clancy's daily *Saratoga Special* provided by far the most informative and colorful writing about the meet, and his book, *Saratoga Days,* was the best I'd ever read about the place.)

I spent a fine night with Pierre Bellocq, as the life-sized fiberglass horse that he had painted in a gaudy blend of racing silk colors brought $31,000 at a charity auction. Allen Jerkens was present, but did not bid. Any horse Jerkens would spend $31,000 on would have to be able to go five-eighths in fifty-seven and change.

On Friday, August 8, Volponi's easygoing half brother, Gentle Nudge, made his Saratoga debut, in a maiden race, at a mile and an eighth. Gentle Nudge, at 25-1, loped easily around the course, never extending himself. He finished thirty-one lengths behind the winner, eight lengths behind the horse closest to him, and ahead only of a horse that did not finish. He jogged back to the barn afterward not tired in the least, and as happy as a schoolboy who'd just enjoyed a period of recess.

"He's got the competitive instinct of a cow in the slaughterhouse," P.G. said the next morning. "I'll give him one more chance, because of his breeding. Then I'll cut the balls off him and sell him to the steeplechase bunch. Maybe he can be trained to jump. He sure can't run."

———

Increasingly, P.G.'s continuation at the game's highest level seemed dependent on Volponi. After the big horse's startling win in the Classic, P.G. had said, "He'll be even better at five." His own faith remained unshaken, but P.G. did concede that four consecutive second-place finishes had taken a bit of wind out of the sails—particularly in terms of sale price.

Not boasting seven-figure breeding himself, and with one knee turned out a bit more than was suitable for classic conformation, Volponi's potential value as a stallion was tied tightly to his performance on the track. There were some on the Saratoga backstretch who estimated privately that Volponi's four straight losses already might have cut his value in half.

But even if he brought only $5 million, instead of $10 million, he was P.G.'s big horse—the first big horse P.G. had ever had—and the quickest way to be sure that P.G. would not speak to you for the rest of the summer, or, perhaps, for the rest of your life, was to disparage Volponi within his hearing.

It was too awkward to talk about openly, but the friends who had known P.G. best and longest would smile and shake their heads and whisper, "The old man has fallen in love with that horse." And it wasn't only because of what he'd done in Chicago. P.G. had loved Volponi from the start.

No matter the sale price, the sight of Volponi entering the van for the one-way ride to Kentucky, or to an airplane for an even longer trip, would cost P.G. more than a little piece of his heart. It would also be a sad day for Mary Kay and for daughters Kathy and Karen and for granddaughter Emma.

"That horse has been the best thing for the Johnson family since the granddaughter was born," one old friend said to me. "And what's she now, fifteen years old?"

P.G. My big problem my whole life was I could never sell myself. I don't have that kind of personality. I'm not a high-society trainer like most of the rich owners want. I'm not gonna waltz around the dance floor and charm the shit out of everybody. Leave me in the barn with the horses and I'll do fine. Give me a little money to buy some horses and I'll do better. I'll treat your horses like kings and queens, but I'm not gonna kiss your ass to keep your business.

That's not the subservient kind of attitude most of the big owners want. It also don't help that I'm a Jew. How many Jews are training horses for the people with the Social Register names, or for those old plantation owners in Kentucky? In New York racing, they put a few Jews in high places for appearances. In Kentucky, they don't even bother to do that.

The biggest owners I had for the longest time were a couple of Jews: Mortie Rosenthal and Al Green. Called themselves Meadow Hill Stable. Rosenthal owned the biggest chain of Jewish funeral homes in the country: He buried every rich Jew from Scarsdale to Miami Beach. Then his brother's daughter married a guy named Steve Ross, and all of a sudden the Rosenthal Funeral Homes are taking over other businesses, one of which was the Kinney parking garages, which they used to buy Warner Communications, which later Ross merged with Time, Incorporated, that got tied in with that AOL Internet thing. See, I bet you never knew that the Internet got started in Mortie Rosenthal's funeral home.

I was with them for twenty-one years, and, Jesus, did we do good. See, how I proved I could breed horses was I made them buy Naskra when he retired and then I had to go find him some mares. These guys didn't want to spend money on mares, so I bought one for three thousand dollars. I found out later I could have bought her for five hundred.

First foal: Nasty and Bold, who won the Brooklyn in '78, setting a stakes record, and then ran third to Affirmed and Alydar in the Travers, and a month later ran third to Seattle Slew and Affirmed in the Marlboro. Second foal: Told, who still holds the world's record for a mile and a sixteenth on the turf. Still holds it, the world's record.

A month before Bee Bee Bee won the Preakness in '72, I spotted his full sister in for thirty thousand dollars at Gulfstream, and I claimed her for Meadow Hill. She runs okay, and we breed her, and once she's in foal to a decent horse they want to sell her in the Keeneland sale. I'm gonna get 10 percent of whatever she brings. They kept asking me what would she bring, and I kept saying, "I don't know." I can evaluate foals better than most people, and yearlings as good as anybody. But a mare in foal who hasn't had produce to the races yet, that depends on who wants her.

Now, there was a guy in Kentucky named Trader Clark. He would buy and sell horses, and somebody recommended to Mortie and Al that they talk to him about what she's worth, so the next thing you know, he invites us to dinner. He had a home almost next to the runway at the airfield across the street from Keeneland, and he had an all-purpose girl, good-looking—man, she was good-looking!—a French girl. She could cook, she could serve drinks, and I imagine she could do everything.

Neither one of these guys could drink. And this is the night before the sale, and they start drinking, and she's barbecuing steaks out in the back. Within an hour, Mortie's on the couch, sound asleep, snoring. The other guy, Al Green, is on the floor. Trader Clark says, "Your boys ain't much drinkers, are they, Johnson?" Then he gets me in the corner and says, "We can make some real money. You got these two Jews, and you and I will bid that thing up, and you and I will split this, we'll split that, we'll do real good."

It was like one o'clock in the morning before I got these two slobs to where they could stagger out to the car. We go back to the Campbell House, where we're staying, and they call me at six o'clock the next morning, and they say, "That Trader Clark is such a nice man. He called us this morning to see how we felt. And he wants to give us three hundred thousand dollars for the mare. He wants to buy her privately."

I said, "Does he? And does he want to let her go through the sale, but if she brings less, that's all you get, but if she brings more he keeps the difference?" "Yeah, that's right." I said, "I don't think I'd do that." "Oh, you're so negative. Why did you even come with us?" I said, "Because you asked me to." So we went around some, and they sold him the mare for four hundred thousand dollars. Then—my joy of joys!—he ran her through the sale and she only brought three hundred thousand, and he tried to welch on 'em. He hadn't given 'em the check yet.

They were screaming at him now, these two tycoons, because he'd told them he'd guarantee the four hundred no matter what she brought in the sale. I said to 'em, "Stop screaming. Get in the car." So they do, and I go over to him, and I says, "Trader Clark, that's what they call you, right?" Now, I never dealt with him before, but I knew him. Everybody knew him. He says, "Yeah, have a cigar." He smoked good cigars. He gave me a cigar. I lit it up. I said, "Either you give me a check for four hundred thousand dollars, or I'm gonna fucking bury you with Bull Hancock and Leslie Combs [two of Kentucky's leading breeders], and whoever the reporter for the *Lexington Herald-Leader* is, he's gonna get the story, too."

He says, "You think I wouldn't pay 'em?" I says, "Of course you wouldn't pay 'em, but you're gonna pay 'em now." He says, "Okay, okay, but I don't know why you're sidin' with the Jews." I said, "Just make out the check to Meadow Hill." And I got the check and took it out to the car and I handed it to them. They said, "How did you do that?" I says, "Leave it alone." I was so disgusted with those assholes.

You know, I'm bad that way. When I know what I'm doing, I know where I'm at—leave me alone to do my job. I could have gone in with that guy, got anything I wanted. "We gotta fuck the Jews." Like what was that famous ship? "We gotta sink the *Bismarck*." It was the same song. "We gotta fuck the Jews." Except he didn't know he was talking to one.

But that's Kentucky. That's the way it is. Beautiful country, gorgeous, gorgeous. They're blessed with the land, all that limestone, the horses eat that grass, it makes them strong, it looks so great. But the people? Boy, I'm gonna tell you— scary.

10 It rained so hard on Sunday, August 10, that one of the races had to be canceled because there was too much water on the track. Even at Saratoga—notorious for its smothering humidity and torrential summer rains—no one could remember that having happened before.

Funny Cide's temperature dropped to 99, but Barclay Tagg was not optimistic. "I'm never optimistic," he said.

Even P.G.'s congenital optimism was being tested.

He started a two-year-old filly named Lass Dance. She finished next to last.

He started a three-year-old colt named I'm A Goer, who finished second.

He started a three-year-old colt named Ramillus, who went off at 36-1 and finished seventh in a field of ten.

He started a three-year-old colt named My Man Alex, who finished last in a field of seven, beaten forty-four lengths, and sixteen lengths behind the sixth-place horse.

The meet was half over. After twelve tries, P.G. still hadn't won a race.

A group of prospective buyers from Japan arrived at the barn one morning. They smiled and bowed and took hundreds of photographs of Volponi as he stood, unruffled, on the grass in front of his stall. The big horse seemed to know that this, too, was part of the job.

"Tell 'em if they have any questions, just ask," P.G. said to an interpreter.

But they didn't. They took hundreds of pictures and quite a few notes and they made frequent comments to one another, but no one from the Japanese group had a single question for P.G.

He shook his head after they left. "You know much about Japanese people?" he asked me.

"Nope."

"How the hell can they fly halfway around the world and then spend only fifteen minutes taking pictures of the horse and not even have any questions?"

"Maybe they figured you wouldn't tell them the truth."

"Nobody ever thinks you're going to tell them the truth about a horse, but that don't stop 'em from asking."

———

To start the second half of the meeting, he ran a four-year-old named Robbie's Rockin, who finished third, at 9-1.

"We do everything for their well-being," P.G. said. "We

have the best blacksmith, Bobby Politto. We have a good vet, Dr. Hunt. There are no great vets, there are good ones. The great ones are the surgeons who don't fuck it up, I guess. Christ, I even bring in Nan Miller, a woman who does acupuncture. You do all that and you have a right to expect something. But some of these horses are totally no good. Absolute losers. I can't help it. I have found, nine out of ten times, the bastards run to their pedigree. If they run at all. Some of them simply can't run.

"I'm probably too goddamned patient. By temperament, I prefer to bring them slowly and still have them when they're four and five. These days, I'm standing alone with an attitude like that. The syndicates have changed the game. The syndicate manager goes to the bank and borrows the money. Then he goes to the sale and buys the horses with the borrowed money. Then he chops the horse up four ways, eight ways, however many. But that horse had better show something at two, because those people want a quick return. And a lot of times you burn the horse out trying to do that. That's where it goes wrong. They want a quick return, but what they get is a broke-down horse, or a laid-up horse.

"There's nothing wrong with running a two-year-old, even early. But putting the pressure on them and breaking them from the gate as hard and fast as they can, that's a different story. You're sure as Christ gonna burn them out. I could give you some names, trainers who look good winning races, but how many horses do they go through? How many do they break down? How much other people's money do they burn?

"I can't do it that way. I'm not a good enough liar. And if you handle horses that way, you sure as hell can't tell your owners the truth. All the owner has to do is count: 'I sent you ten two-year-olds and how many are left a year later?' I can't do it that way, never could. Not so much because of the owners—I just couldn't do it to the horses."

———

Wednesday, August 13, was "Funny Cide Day" at Saratoga. It rained.

Funny Cide was led to the paddock at 11:30 A.M. Because he had never raced at Saratoga, he'd never been to the paddock before. It was the first time most of his fans had seen him, except on television. The consensus was that he looked like a horse. The whole performance acutely irritated Barclay Tagg.

"He's not a circus horse, he's a racehorse," Tagg said. "If you want a circus horse, go to the circus."

At noon, Barclay Tagg and Jose Santos and half a dozen Funny Cide owners sat at a long table and signed posters.

Tagg looked as if he was undergoing a root canal, and sounded as if he would rather have been.

"When are you going to work him?"

"I don't know. I might not. I can't work him on that track right now. It's terrible. I couldn't even walk across it."

"Is he going to run in the Travers?"

"I don't know. I'll either enter him or I won't. If I enter him, he might run. If I don't, he won't."

"Are you enjoying all this?"

"Listen, can you imagine if you were running a business—say, manufacturing beer cans—and people were hanging around all day asking you why do you do this, how do you do that? It would drive you nuts, especially when you're tired all the time."

The party went on, but Funny Cide's fever had replaced Funny Cide Fever as the theme.

P.G. I would buy the mares and make the breedings for Meadow Hill in the '70s, and we just kept rolling out stakes winners. We were winning all kind of races for years. I mean, I could start showing you pictures; you'd be up all night. And then we started to syndicate the best of them. We syndicated Match the Hatch for a million in 1981. But no matter what I gave Rosenthal and Green, it was never enough. They just got nastier and nastier with time.

Do you know why? Because they never put anything into it. They wouldn't spend money, they never tried to learn anything, they wouldn't even come out to the barn in the morning—so they knew they didn't deserve a bit of their success. The better we did, the more unhappy they got. Some psychologist could probably explain it to you in fancy language. All I know is the more I made for 'em, the bigger pricks they got to be.

We went to Mortie's house once for a big party and he's introducing me to everybody as his trainer. Finally, a guy said to me, "When Mortie plays golf, do you have to massage him before or after?" I explained I wasn't a massager. I didn't say anything else, but I saw Mortie at the races a couple of days later and I said, "Don't you ever invite me anyplace again. I don't want to be known as your trainer. If you want to introduce me as your friend, that's okay. Otherwise, keep your invitations." Boy, he didn't like that.

And the best thing I ever did for him was the one he didn't like the most. This started in 1980. Mary Kay and I went to the Museum Ball at Saratoga that year, and I see Henryk de Kwiatkowski and Woody Stephens at the bar. Kwiatkowski was the guy who eventually took over Calumet after the other bastard ran it into the ground, and he had all these stories about himself as some kind of European count with this romantic past history, all of which turned out to be bullshit.

Woody was exactly the opposite. People used to get bored by Woody because he'd talk and talk, but he never said anything that wasn't true. I loved him. Jerkens loved him. A real horseman's horseman: Shit, he won the Belmont five years in a row. Woody probably had more good horses in his career than anybody. But he had told me time and again that of all the good horses he'd ever had, Danzig was the best. He was by Northern Dancer and he only raced three times and won them all but he'd broke down in the spring and now I know they're going to syndicate him.

Woody says, "Have a drink!" He's already, you know,

halfway gone, and Kwiatkowski looked like he was on cloud nine, too. I asked Woody how much they were going to syndicate him for. I'm not going to ask that sap Kwiatkowski, because he stole Polish airplanes and flew them all over the place, and I didn't give a shit about him. Woody says, "Seventy-five thousand a share."

I says, "I'll take one." I wanted one for Meadow Hill. At the time, I couldn't pay that kind of money myself, plus I could never put myself ahead of my owners in something like that. "Well, wait, Woody," says Henriky, "I don't think there's any left." See, he was trying to create a demand before there was one. But Woody says, "Henriky, there's thirty-three left." He was tough that way. He never went along with the bullshit.

So I said, "Put me down for one." And I told Rosenthal and Green, and they were happy to have it. Then I said, "Mortie, you need to buy some mares. The cheap ones you got are not suitable for this horse."

"We're not going to buy any mares," Mortie says. "And by the way I don't like how you got us to buy the share. You've probably got some deal going on the side."

Well, I didn't say nothin' at the time, or ever, but three years later at Saratoga a friend of mine who was involved with the syndicate comes to me and says they want to buy the share back. His first crop had been terrific, and by now everybody in the world wants to breed to Danzig, which they were right about, because he's still going twenty years later and he's sired more than a hundred graded stakes winners. I said, "How much will they pay for the share?" "Seven hundred and fifty thousand." Hmm. That's not a bad return on seventy-five thousand in three years. I said, "You got a deal."

It's about eight o'clock in the morning, and Rosenthal and Green are staying at the Gideon Putnam—that was the Jewish summer home of everybody at Saratoga. They'd gone down to breakfast, so I told Al's wife. (She was a rattle-brained, talk-you-to-death son of a bitch, never knew what she was talking about, in my opinion.) I said, "Tell them I got a lot of money for them if they call me back at the barn inside of an hour." I knew they'd like the sound of that. They called me back in five minutes. I said I could get them seven-fifty for the Danzig share and I'd take 10 percent. "Phil, you're kidding! Phil, you're a genius!" Mortie's screaming at the top of his lungs. It was like they found the fucking Hope diamond.

See, I would've been dead with the horse because I had no mares that were compatible with him, and they wouldn't buy suitable mares, which would have cost a little more than the usual thirty-five hundred that I was allotted to buy a mare. Like I told you, I paid three thousand for the dam of Nasty and Bold. I paid thirty-five hundred for the dam of Match the Hatch. Quiet Little Table's mare cost five thousand. So they were spoiled. They weren't going to spend any money, which was all right. I was happy to take my 10 percent.

Only I just about never got it. I billed them for that 10 percent for months. They wouldn't pay it. Mortie just wasn't going to pay it. I finally had to have somebody connected with the syndicate call him from England and embarrass him—as much as Mortie could be embarrassed. He thought the deal wasn't complete unless he could screw me, too. And that was the beginning of my end with Meadow Hill.

The end of the end was I brought a veterinarian in there, a guy I met in Ocala. Nickname was Pug. He was a little tough Texan bastard. He was a pretty good racetrack vet in Jersey, and I needed a racetrack vet in Ocala because I had racehorses there. I didn't want a broodmare vet: I wanted a racehorse vet.

So we got along good and Rosenthal would come and watch the horses train, and I introduced them, and Doc [Pug] was building a house nearby and Rosenthal had bought a home on the golf course, and they talked a lot. One day Doc came to me and said, "I need a favor. Do you think you could speak up for me to Rosenthal? I need sixty thousand dollars." It was something to do with the house he was building. I said, "Don't ask him. I'll ask him for you, because he'll say no real quick because he doesn't know you that well." So I asked Mortie. He said, "Is the guy all right?" "Yep." "If he doesn't pay it, will you pay it?" "Nope." But he gives him the sixty thousand anyway, and I guess Pug did pay back, because they got chummy.

That was about the time that people started pinhooking

yearlings at the sales. Do you know what that is? It's buying yearlings, breaking and training them, and then selling them as two-year-olds. It's a good business. I couldn't go close to it, because I couldn't get away from Belmont, Aqueduct, and Saratoga, and you can't do both. I can breed, because I don't have to look at those horses every day, but pinhooking you've got to be there on the scene. So Doc started pinhooking on the side for Mortie, and they had a couple of home runs, like they'd buy one for twenty and sell it for seventy-five or a hundred. Not a huge profit, but it was black instead of red.

Now, I had a mare for Mortie. Her picture's hanging by the escalator in the clubhouse at Belmont: Queen Alexandria, a New York–bred stakes winner as a two-year-old. The day she won the stake that the picture's from, she bled out of her nostrils. We had no Lasix in New York in those days, but everybody else did, and after that bleeding she was gonna need Lasix to keep racing.

I said, "Mortie, this mare can win a real stake, open company, not just one for state-breds. Take her to Tampa, I got a trainer for you down there, and you can use Lasix." "What's Lasix?" I explained it to him. She went down there and she won a stake, and I never saw her again.

Churchill Downs, Delaware, all over the place: She won a lot of stakes with Lasix, and I never saw her again. Now, I could've done the out-of-town stuff with her. I raced all the horses I wanted to race on Lasix during the summer. I raced in Maryland, Monmouth, Meadowlands, anyplace, it didn't matter. So right away I knew who was engineering this—keeping the horse away from me—was Doc. He would pick out trainers for her in those different places, and in return they would bring owners in to buy his two-year-olds in training—the kind of thing I never did, and Doc knew it.

By then he was socializing with Mortie on the golf course down there, and I guess eventually he wanted me out of the picture, because one day Mortie called me up and said, "We're going to make a change. We're going with Dutrow as our trainer. He'll be by for the horses in half an hour." And that was it. After twenty-one years, that was it.

11 On the afternoon of Thursday, August 14, a massive power failure struck the eastern United States. Racing was disrupted for only half an hour, but elsewhere in Saratoga Springs electrical service was not restored until late that night.

With my cottage stifling from lack of air-conditioning, I went out in search of an open restaurant. The first place I found still operating was Bruno's, the old bar and grill across from the track's main gate on Union Avenue. Given that its location would have enabled it to thrive in August even if it served only oats and hay, Bruno's wasn't bad for simple fare, and the atmosphere was always cordial. I went in for a couple of beers and a burger and a hard blast of air-conditioning.

Sitting, apparently unnoticed, at a small table along the wall were P.G. and Mary Kay. He motioned for me to join them.

"Don't order the ribs," he said, pushing a nearly full plate to one side.

Like Allen Jerkens, P.G. was a man who knew his restaurants, and he dined most frequently at Sergio's and the Wishing Well north of town. (Jerkens and his wife, along with many other track insiders, favored Il Paradiso on South Broadway, while jockeys tended to bring family and friends to Leon's, a Mexican restaurant owned by former rider Filiberto Leon. The bustling and price-gouging Siro's, a short walk from the racetrack clubhouse, drew mostly tourists with a high tolerance for overcrowding and earsplitting din.)

"This is kind of a drop in class for you, isn't it?" I said.

"It's open," P.G. said. "And it's nice people. Just don't order the ribs."

"I was going to cook at home," Mary Kay said, "but we have no power at all."

I had dined with the Johnsons under slightly more formal circumstances (i.e., I'd been invited) earlier that summer, and it had been a fine occasion. Although hampered by his failing voice, P.G. had been a gracious host, and I'd found Mary Kay's acerbic candor bracing.

At Bruno's, we quickly established the almost giddy camaraderie that tends to arise among those thrown together by blackouts, blizzards, and other such disruptive events. P.G. and Mary Kay lingered over an after-dinner drink while I ordered.

"Is it true," I asked P.G., "that you met Mary Kay at the racetrack?"

"Washington Park, in Chicago," he said, "although the

Disney guys are going to change it to Arlington because of Volponi. They think it's more sentimental if I won the biggest race of my life at the same track where I met my wife fifty years before."

"Fifty-eight years, Phil," Mary Kay said. "Remember, we've been married fifty-seven."

"But why would a beautiful Irish Catholic girl from a fine South Side family like the McMullens take up with a struggling Jewish racehorse trainer?"

"Go to the movie," P.G. said. "You'll find out."

"It was strictly a matter of sex appeal," Mary Kay said.

She saw me glance at P.G., trying to imagine.

"Oh, you'd never believe it to look at him now, but at one time I think Phil was the handsomest man in America. Or at least in Chicago, which was good enough for me."

"Don't believe it," P.G. said. "The truth is, her father was a horseplayer and he was hoping I could give him some winners."

"So, he bartered his daughter for a tip on the double?"

"Don't you believe *that!*" Mary Kay said. "Once I laid eyes on him, I wasn't going to let him get away."

"How'd your parents feel about him being Jewish?"

"Oh, they hated it. But he took the religious instructions and became a Catholic right away."

"You did?" I asked P.G. "You really converted to Catholicism?"

"Sure, what the hell did I care? It's not like I'd ever been religious. I did what I had to do to get the girl."

"Tell him about your so-called religious instruction, Phil," Mary Kay said. "Tell him what that turned into."

"The priest was a horse degenerate. I guess these days that wouldn't be considered so bad. But we were supposed to be studying a catechism, or the Bible, or some damned thing, and once he found out I was a trainer, all he wanted to do was go over the *Racing Form*. This is a true story, not a racetrack story. Father Fisher was his name. I'd get in there every week to learn religion and he'd have the *Racing Form* spread all over his desk, and we'd spend the whole session going over the card. I never did find out what that bird did."

"What bird?"

"He means the Holy Ghost," Mary Kay said. "Phil, don't blaspheme."

"What the hell do you care anymore? You and Kathy walked out about twenty years ago when they started in about abortion and none of us have ever been back, which is fine with me. I was a bad Jew and a worse Catholic. My granddaughter, Emma, she's going to a Quaker school now, and that's fine. I like those Quakers. They don't preach at you. In fact, they spend a lot of time not saying anything. There's some other religions that ought to pick up on that."

"But did he win?"

"Did who win?"

"The priest."

"Hell, yes, he won. I wanted the girl. He had to win."

"We must have had God on our side," Mary Kay said, "because that happened during Phil's one lucky phase as a bettor."

"There's only been one?"

"Yes, and it was brief," Mary Kay said.

"Lasted long enough for me to marry you," P.G. said.

"My own horses weren't worth a damn yet," he said to me. "The only way I could make money was betting. This would have been the summer of '45. I won—I don't know what it was—three, four, five thousand dollars. Enough to get married on, anyway."

"Then your luck changed?"

"Yeah, but I was a stubborn bastard, as well as dumb, so it took me longer than it should have to admit it. It wasn't until I got to be among the leading trainers in Chicago and we were still always broke that I figured it out. Then I realized it was the betting, and I got my wits about me and I quit. I haven't made a serious bet in fifty years."

"Don't start acting proud of yourself, Phil. Tell him what really happened."

"That is what happened."

"Your wits? No, Phil, it was your stomach."

"Well, okay. Kathy was about three years old, and we were living with Mary Kay's parents, and her mother would take care of Kathy when we went to the races in the afternoon. This one day, we said we'd be home late because we were going out to dinner that night. There was a lot of good restaurants in Chicago. But I lost all the money we had betting that day and we didn't have any money for a restaurant.

"On the other hand, we couldn't go home, because I couldn't admit to Mary Kay's parents that I'd lost all our money and that we couldn't afford to eat. So we had to drive around starving until it was late enough so we'd look like we were coming back from the restaurant. And even when we got there we couldn't eat, because supposedly we'd just finished dinner. I went to bed so hungry that night that I got up in the morning and said, never again."

"And you stuck to it?"

"I sure as hell did. With me, eating comes first. Besides, nobody makes money over the long haul betting on horses. I don't care who they are or how many lies they tell you. But I will say this: You know that little filly I showed you a while back, Micmaceuse, the one named after me?"

"Yes."

"She's in the first tomorrow, and it'll probably come off the grass because of the rain, and if it does, there won't be anything left in the race, and she'll win it."

"You're saying I should bet her?"

"I'm not saying anybody should ever bet anything. But here."

He reached into his pocket and took out a twenty-dollar bill.

"To win. For Emma. She's not old enough to go to the window herself."

———

I bet so much on Micmaceuse the next day that she dropped from 10-1 in the morning line to 7-5 at post time. She won laughing. I gave Emma the $49 she had coming as a result of the $4.90 win price and took the rest in a check for an amount so vast that the chairman of the Jockey Club, Ogden Mills Phipps, had to cosign it. I moved out of my cottage and into the Morton Rosenthal Suite at the Gideon Putnam, and I made an offer of $8 million for Volponi, just as a way of giving something back. Even more extravagantly, I bought a round for the house at Siro's.

Well, she won laughing, and paid $4.90, anyway. The rest is a racetrack story.

The important thing was that the win by Micmaceuse enabled P.G. to keep his streak alive. He had now sent out a winner for forty-two consecutive years, something that none of the thousands of other trainers at Saratoga since the nine-teenth century had ever done.

"I guess it's better than having to start over," he said to the journalists who crowded around him as he left the winner's circle, "although I would have been willing to do that, too."

"When did you know you had this race won?"

"About eight o'clock this morning, when they took it off the grass."

"Are you going out to celebrate now?"

"I'm going to the racing secretary's office to scratch Volponi for tomorrow. Now, I don't need him anymore."

Before that news got broadcast, he assured the press that he was kidding. Volponi would run, as planned, in the Saratoga Breeders' Cup Handicap the next day.

"Then I'll have two wins in a row," he said. "I'll have momentum. Pletcher had better watch out."

The joking effectively disguised P.G.'s sense of relief. When you've been in the business for sixty years, and you're in the Hall of Fame, and you won the Breeders' Cup Classic the year before, you can't act as if winning a claiming race means much. But pride dies hard.

It was clear, if not from P.G. himself, then from Kathy and Karen and Emma—and from his assistant, Ocala, and Ocala's wife, Debby, back at the barn—that keeping the streak alive had been important to him.

And when you loved an old man the way those people loved P.G. it became important to you, too, because you cherished every new day he had in the sun.

"You come back next year," Ocala said, displaying a rare grin. "He gonna make it forty-three."

P.G. Let me tell you about Ocala. A long time ago, I started wintering in Ocala, Florida. They got a limestone ridge under the ground there, just like in Lexington. Best places on earth to nourish a horse.

I'm driving along one morning and I see this guy hitch-hiking. He wasn't black, but he wasn't white, either. You never saw many Spanish people in Ocala then. This was the very early seventies, and they hadn't got up there yet. I guess I stopped as much out of curiosity as to be nice.

I opened the door and said, "Where you going?" He didn't speak much English then. He said, "Ocala Stud Farm." He'd been in South Florida, working on a horse farm, and I guess the guy pushed him around and he beat the shit out of the guy, and he got scared that he was gonna get in trouble, not being legal at the time. So he hitchhiked up to Ocala. Seemed like a decent guy—real strong, serious guy—so I gave him a job walking horses, and we got along fine.

This goes on for a couple of years. I develop confidence in him, because he pays attention to everything and he knows how to deal with any problems that come up with the Spanish speakers in the barn, but most of all because I can see what a great instinct he has with the horses.

Now, I had an owner named Tom Whitney. He wasn't one of them—not that kind of Whitney. This guy actually did something for a living. One thing he did was he translated the books that Russian guy wrote, what's his name, not one of the dead guys, the modern one—Solzhenitsyn. You could look that up.

I had some classy owners, you know. They weren't all like Mortie Rosenthal. Maybe they weren't as rich as I would've liked, but they had a life. Whitney, who did Solzhenitsyn, and Bob Irving, who used to run the New York City Ballet orchestra, and I had a big newspaper guy once, Dave Laventhal. He used to run *Newsday* on Long Island, which is how I knew him, and then he went out to L.A., and I never know what happens to anybody once they move to L.A.

When he was still on Long Island, Laventhal and a bunch of guys started a stable. They called it the Qwerty Stable, because that's the letters on the top row of the typewriter: *q-w-e-r-t-y*. It was some kind of newspaper joke. I had a lot of fun with those guys.

Anyway, Tom Whitney—Thomas P. Whitney is the name you'll see on all his Russian books—was up in Connecticut. He had a bookstore in some goddamned town there, and each wife he had—there was two or three of them—worked in the bookstore. But with this one particular wife he owned a couple of horses, and they wanted to get in the breeding business. So they bought a nice three-year-old filly from the Phippses that I recommended as a broodmare. Bubbling, her name was. Beautiful-bred filly—all the Phipps horses are beautifully bred.

They paid a hundred thousand for her and they sent a driver down to bring her up to the farm in Connecticut. They're going to breed her up there, so I'm never going to see her again. That's fine, I'm training racehorses. I hope it works out.

But their driver stopped for dinner in some joint and got half drunk, and then I don't know what the hell happened, but Mrs. Whitney calls me that night, got me out of bed, wanted to know where the horse was. I said, "How do I know? That's your driver, not mine." I knew the horse had left Belmont, because she was signed out, but I didn't know where the hell she was by then.

She calls me again the next morning and says, okay, the horse is there, the guy got there in the middle of the night and led her off the van and put her in a paddock. But she says, "We can't catch her." "What do you mean, you can't catch her?" "I go out with a shank, and my van driver chases her toward me so I can catch her, but I can't."

So I said, "First thing you do is fire that drunken son of a bitch. Then you take her water out and don't feed her. In a couple of days, she'll come over and put her head right on your shoulder."

"Oh, I can't do that to a horse!"

I said, "Okay, in that case, how about I train that horse and race her for you, instead of you start breeding her right away?" She talks to her husband about it, and he says okay. So I said, "I'm gonna send a van up there with a guy on the van and we'll bring the horse back to Belmont Park."

I sent Ocala. He went up there, opened up the van, put the ramp down, took a shank, walked in there: "Come on up here, you son of a bitch!" She walked right up and he put her on the van. He knew how to handle racehorses. She was the gentlest, kindest filly you ever saw, but she had them buffaloed, rearing up there, playing the gorilla, and this guy's chasing her—it's a wonder Mrs. Whitney didn't get killed.

We had a two-year run with her. We won the Gardenia, the big stake for fillies and mares at Garden State, and she won at Saratoga, and Ocala was the guy who took care of her. It was his first decent horse he handled all by himself, and he did it so good that after that he became my top assistant. But you know something? I never picked up another hitchhiker. You got to know how to quit when you're ahead.

I always did good in Florida, though. One year, I'm down at Hialeah. If you remember, there's a train track runs right by

Hialeah. In the old days we used to bring horses in that way, and the Palm Beach train came down with the big shots. Then freight took over. One day, I'm leaving my barn. It's eleven o'clock in the morning. I go out the stable gate, look to my left, I want to go that way, but there's a fuckin' freight train sittin' there. So I keep goin' straight, lookin' left every block, and finally I see the end of the train, the caboose, so I make a left to go back toward Palm Avenue.

On the street I turned on to, there was these little houses, and in the front yard of one of them there was a horse. Now, what the fuck is a horse doing in Hialeah, other than at the racetrack? It's runnin' around in circles, just playin', like horses will do, and it looks like a Thoroughbred. Nobody is in there, it's just him. So I pull over to watch him for a while, because I like to watch horses. And here comes this guy with a mailbag over his back, but it's empty, so I know he's not delivering the mail. He opens the gate and he steps into the yard: Turns out it's his house, he lives there.

I says, "I just stopped to look at your horse, Mister." He says, "Are you over there at Hialeah?" I said, "Yeah, I'm a trainer. What's that you got over there?" He says, "Well, I bought an old broodmare and she was in foal and she had the baby, and then the price of feed went up, so I gave her away and kept the colt."

I said, "How old is he?" This was right after we went down

in November. Tropical was still running. January 15th is when Hialeah opened for racing. He said, "January 1st, he'll be a two-year-old." I said, "Has he ever had a saddle on his back?" He said, "Yeah, but he's wild. Wait, I'll get him." So he goes and gets a rope with a snap on the end of it, but this horse had his number—running around with his tail up in the air, rearing up, playing. I said, "I'll come back someday when you catch him."

I started to walk away, but I stop and turn around and say, "Do you want to sell him?" "Yeah, I want to sell him." "How much do you want for him?" He said, "Well, you're a trainer, you tell me." I said, "Oh, don't put me in that spot. You walk with those fucking sore feet all your life." My Uncle Izzy was a mailman in Chicago, on the West Side, and he was hurtin' all the time, and the Jews aren't supposed to have to work like that.

I say, "Does he have any papers?" "Yeah, I gave the mare away but I kept all her papers." Now, who would take the mare but not care about the papers? Probably some Cubans, who chopped her up and ate her. Anyway, I gave him seven hundred fifty dollars for the horse, and he gave me the horse and the papers.

I named him Letter Carrier, which made the mailman very happy, and I walked him back down along the road to the track. Problem was, it's the worst nutrition in the world,

South Florida, for a horse. The grass is no good. He bucked his shins, he popped a knee, and I couldn't run him for more than a year.

He was just a cheap claimer, but eventually he won a couple. One day—and I still got the picture—he wins with Hartack by eight lengths at Arlington. And that was the big apple in those days. Letter Carrier: They should've put him on a stamp.

12 I'd spent so much time with P.G. that I'd gotten used to the sound of his voice. But one day I went to the Museum of Racing across Union Avenue from the track, and I listened to the remarks he'd made upon his induction into the Hall of Fame in 1997.

The difference was unsettling. Then, he sounded slightly hoarse. Now, it was as if he had a permanent case of laryngitis, or worse.

"It'll clear up once I get back to Florida," he said. "It's been ten years since I've wintered down there. Mary Kay doesn't want me to go, because she doesn't think I should be on my own, and she doesn't want to go with me because she doesn't like to travel anymore. But I'll be fine. I'll bring Ocala; we'll share a condo down there. Palm Meadows, that new training operation, is supposed to be state-of-the-art. I've spent too many god-damned winters in the cold. It's time for Florida again."

This had become his favorite refrain. And again he smiled, anticipating: "I'll watch the new two-year-olds develop, get out to dinner again with Jerkens and Barclay, and let that sun shine on these vocal cords, so I can come back next year sounding like a human being."

In the absence of Mineshaft and Medaglia d'Oro, and because Jerry Bailey would be riding him, Volponi seemed certain to be the heavy favorite in the Saratoga Breeders' Cup Handicap. Only Harlan's Holiday, trained by Todd Pletcher, seemed a threat.

Harlan's Holiday had been a distant ninth to Volponi in the 2002 Classic, but so far this year he'd won the Donn Handicap at Gulfstream, had finished second in the $6 million Dubai World Cup in March, and in July had run second to Congaree in the $750,000 Hollywood Gold Cup. Pletcher's regular jockey, John Velazquez, the only rider who'd won more races than Bailey at the Saratoga meet, would ride him.

But P.G. was exuding a confidence to which he had only aspired before the Whitney. He seemed to harbor no doubts that his big horse would reduce Harlan's Holiday, and the rest of the field, to chopped liver—or its equine equivalent.

Dark gray clouds clogged the sky on Saturday, sealing in the oppressive humidity. The temperature remained in the mid-80s. Showers began in mid-afternoon. The Saratoga Breeders' Cup Handicap was the seventh race of the day, post time 4:30 P.M.

Besides Harlan's Holiday, three other horses in the field of eight were attracting mild attention from bettors:

Puzzlement—the Allen Jerkens horse that P.G. had said he feared more than Medaglia d'Oro in the Whitney.

Iron Deputy—who had sprinted away from Volponi on a sloppy track in the mile-and-an-eighth Brooklyn Handicap at Belmont in June, and who had held on to win. Subsequently, Iron Deputy had finished out of the money at Arlington. Trained by Allen Jerkens's son, Jimmy Jerkens, he'd be ridden by—of all people—Jose Santos. *Mundo pequeño* or, as they say in English, small world.

Blue Boat—a recent European import trained by, *mundo pequeño*, Bobby Frankel. Since being put in Frankel's care, Blue Boat had won three consecutive races. This would be his first stakes—a big jump in class—and he'd never before run a mile and a quarter on the dirt, but Bobby Frankel was Bobby Frankel, and in the absence of Bailey he had engaged Saratoga's leading rider of 2002, Edgar Prado.

This added yet another wrinkle, for P.G. had told me that Prado had sought the mount on Volponi after Santos had been dismissed. His agent had pressed P.G. hard until the choice of Bailey was announced. There was nothing unusual about that, but Prado apparently had come by P.G.'s barn a few days later, and had told some of P.G.'s Spanish-speaking help that the choice of Bailey had been a mistake, and that P.G. was going to regret it.

Prado was not known to be mean-spirited or vindictive. To the contrary, he was both popular and respected. A 36-year-old Peruvian, he'd led all riders in the United States in races won in 1997, 1998, and 1999, and his horses had won more than $18 million in purses in 2002, putting him second only to Bailey in that category. It did not seem plausible that he'd get into a snit because P.G. had chosen Bailey instead of him to ride Volponi, but egos were fragile at the game's highest level, and competitive spirit was fierce.

I watched the afternoon's races from a table in the restaurant on the highest floor of the clubhouse. I sat with Pierre Bellocq's youngest son, Remi, and his wife, Bridget. Remi, the executive director of the national Horsemen's Protective and Benevolent Association, was a skilled amateur rider who had once won a race at the San Siro in Milan.

Rain began to fall heavily as the horses approached the starting gate, then just as quickly tapered to a drizzle. The humidity must have been 100 percent, but I had no doubt that I was perspiring as much from nervousness as from the weather. In the two weeks since the Whitney, P.G. had come to seem almost a friend, and I had at least a glimmer of how much it would mean to him to have Volponi finally win another race. A victory would be not only an emotional lift, but would put a more stable floor under the prospective sale price.

———

The big horse looked well, and, as always, Jerry Bailey seemed to brim with confidence in the saddle. P.G.'s new team was heavily favored in the betting, the odds flashing back and forth between even money and 4-5. Harlan's Holiday was at 5-2, Puzzlement at 7-1, Blue Boat at 8-1, and Iron Deputy at 12-1, while the other three entrants ranged from 35-1 to 70-1.

Perhaps the biggest innovation I had found on my return to Saratoga was the ubiquity of television screens: from giant overhead models spaced throughout the grandstand and clubhouse to computer-screen-sized monitors in each box, and at each table in the fanciest restaurants. These had rendered the once indispensable pair of binoculars irrelevant, though many owners and trainers continued to use them, out of either habit or affectation.

I found myself blessing the intrusion of the TV screen, for my hands were trembling so hard by post time that I wouldn't have been able to focus binoculars. I was so nervous I felt queasy. This was the sort of high—an anxiety high, rather than one linked to ecstasy (with or without the eponymous drug)—that I'd experienced prior to every race on which I bet thirty years earlier. Until this moment on my return, however, such intensity had eluded me—a change attributable, no doubt, to my being sixty instead of twenty-eight, as well as to the fact that my once-frantic wagering was now desultory and occasional.

Confident of Volponi's chances, but knowing he'd go off at a price not worth the risk of a simple win bet, I'd put him as the top horse in three exactas, matching him with Puzzlement, Blue Boat, and Iron Deputy.

In an exacta, one must select the first two finishers in proper order. My thinking was that Volponi was nearly certain to win, but if one of the three other viable contenders beat out Harlan's Holiday for second place, I'd get a decent return.

"But you didn't play it both ways?" Remi asked.

"Why would I want to do that?"

"Oh, just in case Volponi runs second, the way he has in every race so far this year."

Remi was a lovely guy. He was bright and funny and personable, and I had known him since he was about seven years old and pretending to be a jockey as he hunched astride the back of his parents' living-room couch. I'd made a winning bet for Remi (though not for myself) on Loud, in the 1970 Travers, because he was too young to go to the window himself, and his father was too busy sketching artificial aristocrats in the paddock.

"What did you bet?" I asked him.

"Puzzlement to win," he said. "Allen Jerkens has brought him up to this one perfectly. Then I made a trifecta box with Puzzlement, Volponi, and Iron Deputy. I don't think Blue Boat has the class for these, and I think Harlan's Holiday is past his peak, at least for this year."

Those were sensible bets—insofar as any bet on a horse race could be termed sensible—but Remi was at the disadvantage of not being close to P.G., and therefore did not know how confident P.G. was.

Then they were off.

After rearing up in the starting gate, Volponi broke well. As expected, Blue Boat went to the front immediately. Bailey, as acclaimed for his cerebral approach to his craft as for his exceptional physical skills, moved Volponi alongside, not trying to take the lead, but staying close.

This meant that Volponi rounded the first turn on the outside, forced to cover more ground than he would have if Bailey had opted for a position along the rail.

They continued that way well into the backstretch: Blue Boat never leading by much more than a length, and Volponi pressing him on the outside. Iron Deputy had been third all the way, with Harlan's Holiday fourth, and Puzzlement, as was his style, at the back of the pack.

On the far turn, with just over a quarter mile to go, Blue

Boat began to falter. Sensing the chance to break the race open, Bailey asked Volponi for his run and the big horse moved to pass Blue Boat on the outside.

With strong, fluid, lengthening strides, Volponi surged up alongside the tiring pacesetter and seemed ready to run clear. Then, just at the quarter pole, Blue Boat suddenly veered hard to the outside, jockey Prado apparently unable to keep his horse on a straight path.

Blue Boat bumped Volponi hard as Volponi tried to go past him, knocking the big horse off stride, and forcing Bailey to take him even wider to avoid further contact.

At the same time, Santos, aboard Iron Deputy, moved out from the rail, creating space for a horse to move inside him. That horse was Puzzlement, who burst through the sudden gap and swept to the lead.

Volponi recovered from the bump, but had been forced so far outside that he'd lost too much ground to make up. He continued bravely down the stretch, and easily held off Iron Deputy for second place, but Puzzlement charged home on the inside to win by more than three. Blue Boat faded to sixth, while Harlan's Holiday, who had never been a factor, finished last, hurting himself in the process.

Puzzlement paid $15.80 to win, and the $2.00 trifecta of Puzzlement, Volponi, and Iron Deputy returned $208.50. The $2.00 exacta of Puzzlement and Volponi was worth $34.40, but I simply could not have bet it that way. It would have been disloyal.

I left the table and worked my way through the crowd to the paddock. One of the many cruel aspects of the racing life is that sometimes it doesn't even give you time to lick your wounds. For P.G. this loss must have been even worse than the Whitney, because in the Whitney Volponi had at least been beaten by a horse widely considered among the best in the world.

Yet even after such a wrenching disappointment, P.G. had to head immediately back to the paddock for the saddling of Belles Lettres, a four-year-old filly he had entered in the next race.

I knew he must have pictured himself approaching the paddock from the winner's circle triumphantly, accepting congratulations from friends like Jerkens and Barclay Tagg, and even from fans who might have recognized him: the short, stooped man in the raincoat, walking slowly but with a resplendent smile on his face.

Instead, for the fifth straight time, he'd have to try to explain why Volponi had finished second again.

By the time I reached him, Belles Lettres had been saddled, and the jockey was already aboard. P.G. looked at me and shrugged.

"He got taken pretty wide," I said.

"He also took a hell of a bump," P.G. said. "Watch it again, in slow motion, when you can. Bailey said he almost went down."

"What do you think happened?"

"I think Prado was mad I didn't give him the mount, and he didn't want me to win with another rider. I'm not going to say that to the press, of course, because they'll say I'm just a sore loser again, making up excuses for my horse."

"But you think Prado bumped him on purpose?"

"Let's see how the horse is in the morning. That'll tell you how hard it was, and maybe how deliberate. Look, whatever Prado might have said at my barn he said in Spanish, and I didn't hear it myself. But you ask Ocala. And look at the replay a few times, in slow motion."

"What are you going to do about it?"

"Nothing. It's part of the game. Horse racing might look pretty from a distance, but up close we're gouging each other's eyes out. That's the game. That's racing. It's the kind of thing that happens every day. As long as the horse is all right, I'll be fine. Now let's go see what Bells can do."

I went with him to his box and watched Belles Lettres, at 7-2, finish eleventh in a twelve-horse field. Then he went home, and so did I.

P.G. Most of my horses have been too slow, but once in a while you get one that's too fast. The heart is there, but the head isn't, and if you bring them on too soon they'll break down, sure as hell. Maplejinsky was like that. She was a Nijinsky filly, and when I first got her, she was too fast for me to run her.

In 1986, I paid seven hundred and fifty thousand dollars of Howard Kaskel's money for her—which was not the kind of thing I ever did before or since, with anybody's money—and every other trainer, including Wayne Lukas, said I was a dumb asshole. "You can't breed long to short—distance horses to sprinters—and you can't do this and you can't do that."

I took her to Saratoga in '87, and I'm trying to get her ready to run, and after her first work up there even Pete, the little fat clocker that's on the training track, said, "Phil, she's faster than anything you've ever had!" I said, "What did she do?" Four furlongs in forty-seven on the Oklahoma training track. A horse hadn't gone that fast in twenty years. She came back and her fucking eyes were bugging out of her head, she was so fired up. I kept her in training, but lightly. You couldn't work her lightly, though. As soon as you worked her, the eyes popped. She wouldn't hold back, and she couldn't be held back.

You had to lie to Kaskel because he had too many advisers. So I called him from Belmont after Labor Day and I told him she'd bucked her shins. See, I had Jerry Goswell down at Fair Hill, in Maryland. It was a training center, and a place for horses to winter. They had a wood-chip track and lots of other good stuff, and I knew Jerry would be just right for her.

Kaskel says, "Well, she won't be out long. So-and-so tells me that's only thirty days." That's what I mean about his advisers. "Oh," I says, "Howard, she really bucked them. I sent her to Jerry Goswell in Fair Hill. We'll bring her up in March." Of course, she was fine, but if I hadn't of lied, she wouldn't have been, because everybody would have tried to pressure me into running her too soon.

Jerry trained her lightly down there through the winter, and she settled down, and when she came back up in March, I could start to do something with her. I got Cordero: best fucking race rider of his era. He'd been in Florida for the winter, and I said, "Angel, you gotta work this horse." His first time on her he comes back and says, "She's mine!"

She was favored in her first start because she'd been working so fast. Phipps had an entry in the race and one of his horses broke its leg and fell, and she jumped over her, didn't get hurt, but that cost her the race; she got beat a neck. I ran her back; she broke her maiden. Then she won an allowance race. I wanted to run her in the Monmouth Oaks, a mile and an eighth, the first part of July. But I couldn't get a prep race, nothing would fill, so I put her on the turf, a mile and a quarter.

There had never been a Nijinsky born that couldn't run on the turf. But she couldn't run on the turf. Not a yard. She was 3-5. I put Julie Krone on her because Cordero couldn't ride her; he was riding a Phipps horse out of town. She finished fourth, a terrible fourth, beaten twenty lengths. "She don't wanna run on the grass," Julie squeaks at me. And Kaskel says, "What are we going to do with her?" I says, "Don't worry about it."

I said, "Angel, I'm gonna work her once and then run her in the Monmouth Oaks." He says, "Good, I'll go down and ride her." His brother-in-law was his agent at that time, and it turned out he had to ride another Phipps horse that day. They gave me like five days' notice, which didn't make me very happy, but Angel says, "I can't help it."

Drew Mollica was Chris Antley's agent. I said, "Drew, you wanna ride in the Monmouth Oaks?" "Oh, for you, for you I'll do anything." You know that bullshit. "I love you. You don't understand how I love you. You're my favorite trainer, blah-blah-blah." You get a lot of that from jockey agents. Anyway, I put Antley on the horse.

It rained like a motherfucker. Rained all night and all day. I sent Ocala down. We had two horses in at Belmont and I stayed with them. They showed a simulcast of the Monmouth race on that big screen they used to have in back of the box seats at Belmont. She won by three, but it looked like it had been even easier than that. I said, "Okay, the next stop is gonna be the Alabama." I'd always wanted to win the Alabama, and I'd never run a horse in it. That's the oldest filly and mare race in the United States: It's not just a race, it's a history lesson. And now I got what I think is a chance.

And of course Antley's gonna ride her. Of course, he's gonna ride her. We go to Saratoga. About a week before the race, she's training brilliant, and I get an idea. I talked it over with Ocala. I always talk things over with Ocala, and with Mary Kay and Kathy and Karen—you know, the family.

I say, "I'm gonna ride Cordero on this filly." "Oh, you can't do that, what about Antley?" Antley had a great personality, like all schizophreniacs or psychopaths or whatever he was. And he was whatever he was big-time, and he died like one of them. Got murdered out in California, or a suicide, I don't think they ever figured it out.

But everybody loved him. He'd hug me, "Oh, God, I'd ride any horse for you. Blah-blah-blah-blah." Now, Kaskel's staying at the Jewish palace, the Gideon Putnam. I called him and said, "I'm gonna put Cordero on her." He said, "Oh, I'll look bad for taking a jockey off after he wins." That's the first thing he thought of: He'll look bad.

He's a nice man: a simple soul, even with all that money. His father came first, you know, and it can't always be easy knowing your father was the one who made the money. When he had the golf tournament—he had that big golf course at his hotel in Florida, the Doral—I'd stay there when I'd fly down for the sales. And in the lobby, overhanging everything, was this big picture of his father, frowning down. All those guys used to say, "Howard, he's looking at you like that because you're throwing all his money away buying horses."

So I said, "I'll take the blame. Just tell 'em your trainer's crazy." Then I go to Cordero. I call him over. I say, "Angel, you want to ride this filly?" "Yeah, I'd love to ride her. What are you gonna do with Drew?" He didn't say, "What are you gonna do with Antley?" It was, "What are you gonna do with Drew?" I says, "Fuck Drew." I wasn't cheatin' the owner, right? Here's the leading rider, Cordero; at that time it was like eleven straight years at Saratoga. He puts people over the fuckin' *rail* and his number don't even come down.

Next morning, Drew comes walking by. I call him over. He says, "Yes, Phil. What can I do for you?" I said, "Maplejinsky got a new rider. It's gonna be Cordero." "*What?*" He starts runnin' around in circles. He was screaming and runnin' around and runnin' around. And naturally everybody's standing along the rail, glued to this. You cannot be alone at Saratoga. And he just screamed and he hollered, and finally he even called Mary Kay. "You know what your husband did to me? He took food outta my kid's mouth." This guy, you give him blackface, he coulda been the second Al Jolson.

But it gets settled, and the race comes up, and it's a beautiful day. One of those days that makes you think Saratoga's not so bad, after all. We're down in the paddock, and the whole Kaskel family was there, and every one of them was nice. Lovely wife—a queen. The daughter was nice, son was a nice guy, all of them. Cordero comes up and says, "Poppy, what we gonna do?" I said, "We gotta be in front the whole way." He says, "Okay, unless I fall off at the gate."

She breaks perfect, on the lead. Charlie Whittingham had brought the favorite in from California, Goodbye Halo; belonged to that asshole hardhead Hancock—not Seth, the other one, Arthur. Whittingham was the only outspoken Jew-hating trainer that that guy would ever use. And this filly had won the Kentucky Oaks and everything.

Scotty Schulhofer had a filly in the race, Make Change, and he had Pat Day on her. Pat Day had found God a couple years before that. They were a good team, but we were in front. The pace started out slow—three quarters in twelve, the mile in thirty-seven—but then they got into it and it wound up the second-fastest Alabama ever run.

Coming into the stretch, we were still on the lead, but it was tight with Pat Day's filly. They were head to head, but Cordero's got that cool, he just sits there. Oh, he can get busy, but he gets busy gradually. He doesn't go from sitting still to "Whoo! Whoo! Whoo!"

You know, big, strong, good horses—Volponi is one of them, and Funny Cide is another—cannot handle the jockey going from doing nothing to getting all over them too fast. Their first instinct is to resist: They're not the kind of horses you can push around like that. They throw their head up, they don't want any part of it. You watch races and you'll see why a jock gets removed. A good trainer won't stand for that.

But now Pat Day is starting to ride. He's slow and gradual, like Cordero, and I know when Pat gets busy, Angel is gonna start to hit her, which he should, because she's tough and she'll go. And she does, and she wins by a neck. Jesus, was I happy. This was the *Alabama*! Kathy was sitting with me and Mary Kay, and I said, "Let's get our picture taken with the best mare I ever trained."

Kathy says, "Don't go downstairs yet." "Why?" See, Kathy's a good race watcher. She's got those little opera glasses. She said, "There's going to be an inquiry." I said, "What do you mean there's gonna be an inquiry? We were on the lead all the way." "Cordero hit that filly next to him on the head with his stick." I said, "He did? I didn't see that."

No sooner had I said that than the objection sign goes up. Pat Day claimed foul. And it was up there forever. Forever. But they didn't explain—they kept showing you the head-on shot, and we clearly won. They don't explain why there's an objection, but you could see it if you knew. And Day knew what was going on. I honestly didn't think it made the difference between winning and losing. For me, if they went around again we're gonna win. So finally they made it official, and we all went down, and everybody got their picture taken.

Cordero's eyes, they're rollin' around and almost poppin' out of his head the way the filly's eyes used to. He walks by me and goes, "Ohhhh, shit," and he's grinnin' so hard I think his teeth are gonna fall out of his mouth. And Day, well, I hope he lodged an objection with God later, because he was entitled.

Angel had got away with another one. If you watched the rerun, you could see it. He didn't slash at her, but he tapped her on the chin, hoping to throw her off stride. He knew what he was doing. Angel always did. And he got away with it. And we win.

13 "He's sore as hell," P.G. said of Volponi at the barn the next morning. "That bump was worse than it looked. But his legs seem okay. I'll get Nan out here to give him a treatment tomorrow. She can do some acupuncture, maybe, and she does chiropractic stuff, too. Then, in a couple of days, I'll jog him. He's tough. He should be fine."

"What's next for him?"

"I don't know. I'm not sure what the hell to do now. Maybe I'll put him back on the grass. There's a grass race coming up at Belmont. If he goes good there, I could run him in the Breeders' Cup Turf. That's got a purse of two million, and no trainer has ever won the Classic and that one, too. I'll think about it."

"Will you keep Bailey on him?"

"I can't. Frankel's got the call on him for Medaggily, and I need a guy now who can stay with Volponi the rest of the way. Besides, I just found out that Bailey hurt himself water-skiing last week, and he wasn't riding at full strength on the weekend. He didn't say anything because he didn't want to lose any big mounts. After he lost my race, and then lost the Alabama on Frankel's horse, he makes the announcement: He's taking a couple of days off. I wish one of them had been yesterday. But I'm not saying he cost me the race, because he didn't."

"So who's next?"

"You know, I got thinking about Cordero. If I can't have him, maybe I should use his jock."

"You mean John Velazquez?" Cordero was the agent for the meet's leading rider, John Velazquez.

"Why not? Johnny rode him in the first stakes he ever won, and I get Cordero's smarts tossed in for free."

———

P.G. had one starter on Sunday, a maiden named Bring to Order. She finished ninth.

I didn't go to the track that afternoon, but 71,337 people did—at least that was the number of paid admissions the turnstiles recorded. No special race drew the crowd: It was the giveaway of a commemorative Saratoga wall clock. They later sold for up to twenty dollars on eBay.

Four days later, after Missy Kiri finished tenth in a $50,000 claiming race, P.G.'s second-best horse, She's Got the Beat, romped home in a $58,000 allowance, giving P.G. his second win of the meet. She was ridden by Volponi's new jockey, John Velazquez.

All week Barclay Tagg had been saying he was almost certain that Funny Cide would not run in the Travers: "I don't see anything that is going to make me want to run him. There's nothing to tempt me. It's probably too late. And it's no fun having people ask you all about it every morning. I wish I could just make everybody leave me alone."

There was a story in the newspaper about the pressure Barclay Tagg was under. Saratoga officials and Funny Cide's owners desperately wanted the horse to run, but Tagg did not feel he was ready. Many trainers expressed sympathy for Tagg's plight. The only one who didn't was Bobby Frankel. "Why should I feel sorry for him?" Frankel said. "How can you feel sorry for someone who won the Derby and the Preakness? Forget about it. That's the way it is."

Soon enough, Bobby Frankel was feeling sorry for himself again. On Thursday night, he declared Empire Maker out of the Travers. He said the move was "precautionary" after the horse had developed a slight cough.

Hours later, Barclay Tagg officially scratched Funny Cide, leaving in shreds what had loomed as the biggest race in Saratoga history.

Ninety percent of the game is disappointment.

Ninety percent of the speculation about the real reason for Empire Maker's scratch had to do with the rumors of added security being assigned to Frankel's barn—security that would have made it more difficult for him to administer any unapproved medication to the horse. No officials confirmed or denied anything, and insofar as I knew, none were asked to do so. At the racetrack, most people freely choose to live in a world of gossip and rumor and innuendo. It seems to be part of the mystique.

———

On August 23, despite the absence of both Funny Cide and Empire Maker, Travers Day drew a record crowd of more than 61,000. Perhaps life—or at least Saratoga—was a carnival after all.

If so, Frankel was not among the merrymakers. The day before the Travers, his 1-5 favorite, Wild Spirit, lost a $400,000 Grade I stakes race to an Allen Jerkens filly that was ridden by Jose Santos. And on the big day itself, Frankel was 0 for 7. Peace Rules, his remaining horse in the Travers, finished second to California import Ten Most Wanted. Meanwhile, in California, Medaglia d'Oro lost at Del Mar.

The Whitney, in fact, had been Frankel's last win. Since then, the trainer who could not be beaten in Grade I stakes had lost seventeen consecutive races. Rumor was rampant at Saratoga that the change in fortune was not simply bad luck.

"They've had twenty-four-hour surveillance of his barn

since the Whitney," one trainer told me. "Whatever he was doing, he had to stop."

Naturally, I asked P.G. about this. "Oh, I hear that. I hear a lot of things. But I don't know. It's enough trouble watching my own horses without keeping an eye on Bobby Frankel's. Maybe it's just his personality rubbing off."

Even Frankel acknowledged the rumors. The *Albany Times-Union* reported that while in California, "he was told of whispers that security was beefed up at his Saratoga barn, the implication being that extra eyes were there to make sure no horses were given illegal medications."

Frankel said he was insulted. "The rumor was that I didn't win the Travers because there was security at my barn," he said. "What am I gonna do? If I win, people try to find reasons why I'm winning. If I lose, they try to find reasons why I lose. I can't win either way. With me, you lose when you win and you lose when you lose. Instead of people wanting to come up to my level, they want to drag me down to theirs. That's the way life goes. People try to drag you down. After three years, I'm having a little bit of a slump. It happens to everyone. All you can do is ride it out."

With that, at least, P.G. might have agreed. At best, his entire Saratoga season had been a slump. And all he could do was ride it out until the end. He started four more horses. None won. One was even claimed, but P.G. didn't raise a hand toward the offender. His bare-knuckled Doc Boyens days were behind him.

———

The rain stopped, the humidity dropped, the nights grew cool. P.G. went home two days early. His horses had won only two of twenty-three races, neither a stakes. He hadn't won a stakes race all year. His big horse now had been beaten five times in a row. I didn't know what the sale price might have sunk to, but I observed that prospective buyers had stopped coming around.

"Maybe I'll see you in California," P.G. said. "Breeders' Cup is the last weekend in October."

His voice had weakened since July. The days were growing shorter. The years already had.

2 Belmont

1 I was living in exile. As Harriet Rubin wrote in *Dante in Love,* "Exile is the death of identity . . . Home, career, history: all that defines a man suddenly seems an illusion." True in Dante's time, true in 2003.

The sad ending, by divorce, of a marriage that had lasted more than twenty-five years had deposited me in Southern California in 2002. But not in the semitropical paradise that most people think of when they envision "Southern California."

I was living in a crowded, crumbling city with a population of 120,000. Many signs were in Spanish or Korean. Bail-bond offices and pawnshops and used-furniture stores dominated the downtown. My house was located halfway between Disneyland and the Richard Nixon Museum: 7.8 miles from each.

I lived, in fact, along the Concrete Corridor: a smog-bound, freeway-strangled expanse that stretches east from the cargo ports of San Pedro and Long Beach toward the inland infernos of Fontana, Riverside, and San Bernardino.

I was there because the woman with whom I was living

had to live in the area, because of her position at a nearby university.

It was a tough place to come back to from Saratoga. First, there was the weather. September was always sublime in Saratoga Springs, as I knew from having lived due east and not far from there for more than twenty years.

September in Southern California, however, is every bit as hellish as are July and August. The sun glares, the heat sears, the foul air chokes. And even beyond the weather, after six weeks of living on a human scale, I found it hard to readjust to an area where the population seemed to double monthly, and where SUVs mated openly in shopping-center parking lots. People who thought Saratoga was crowded in August had clearly never been to northern Orange County.

The truth is, I didn't adjust. I stayed indoors with the air-conditioning on and watched TVG–The Interactive Horse Racing Network—all day long. I watched races from Belmont, because that's where everyone from Saratoga had gone, and I missed them, even the ones I'd never met. But I also started watching races from Suffolk and Calder and Delta and Fairplex and Mountaineer and Prairie Meadows and Hoosier and Turfway. I didn't know which track it was half the time, and I didn't know where half of them were, and I never knew who was running, and I certainly didn't care who won. I didn't bet. I just sat: staring at the screen, staying out of the traffic and out of the smog and out of the heat.

TVG flung out races by the dozens, bouncing the viewer from track to track, time zone to time zone, climate to climate even faster than the payoffs could be posted. For gamblers, it was the equivalent of the slot machines the tracks were so frantic to install. For me, the effect was more like that of a morphine drip. Hours would pass as I drifted in and out of consciousness. By the time I was aware that the nightly switch from Thoroughbreds to quarter horses had taken place, it was time for bed.

At first, I thought being back in Orange County was causing my fugue state, and undoubtedly it played a part. But a therapist told me I also was suffering from EDS, the Saratoga strain of which was particularly virulent. EDS—a biological cousin of Funny Cide Fever—is Equine Deprivation Syndrome: a dispiriting malady triggered by sudden loss of up-close access to Thoroughbred horses.

For weeks, I had lived a five-minute drive from the Saratoga stable areas, a five-minute walk from the track. Now, a five-minute drive would take me about a hundred yards in the direction of the Jack in the Box and El Pollo Loco fast-food stands on Imperial Highway. And a five-minute walk was out of the question until November, when the air quality just might improve to only "moderately unhealthy."

TVG was my life-support system, my only connection to the world I'd returned to in July and was finding so hard to leave. The truth was I did not want to leave it. Racing had fallen far over the past thirty years, but the same could fairly have been said about me. I had needed the game in my teens and twenties, and now, at the start of my sixties, I was finding that I needed it again.

The racetrack had been my first refuge from loneliness as I had entered my teens, as it had been P. G. Johnson's refuge from his stepmother. It had attracted my father in ways about which he'd felt so guilty that he was never able to speak to me about them.

I was no longer so drawn by the gambling. What I had found enthralling once again were the horses, and the quirky, idiosyncratic men and women—P. G. Johnson chief among them—who devoted their lives to helping those horses achieve the most from their abilities.

Except for the fact that I didn't smoke, I could easily see myself joining up with the ragged band of old men for whom the horses were a reason—in many cases, the only reason—to get out of bed every day. I took a fresh look at my surroundings: Disneyland and the Nixon Museum, yes, but I was also within forty-five minutes of both Santa Anita and Hollywood Park. And within arm's reach of TVG.

I set up my *Daily Racing Form* Web page so it would notify me a day in advance every time a horse of P.G.'s was due to run. Not that there were that many, and not that most ran any better at Belmont than they had at Saratoga, but it was a way of feeling that I was staying in touch.

———

Naturally, I kept a sharp eye out for Volponi. P.G. entered him in the $200,000 mile-and-an-eighth Grade II Breeders' Cup Handicap at Belmont. The race would be run on Saturday, September 13. It would be Volponi's first grass race of the year. I spoke to P.G. on Friday night. His voice had weakened to the point that it was hard to hear him on the phone.

"The grass course is in good shape," he said. "Tomorrow's supposed to be cloudy, but no rain. He shouldn't have any problem. You know, I ran him in this race a year ago. He finished second. That was his fourth race in a row on grass. Then I put him back on the dirt and he ran second at the Meadowlands, and then he won the Classic. I think the grass should freshen him. And it would be nice to finally win one, get that monkey off his back."

"And yours."

"I don't give a shit. I just want the horse to get some respect."

To my unpracticed eye, it didn't look like there was much in the race that could threaten Volponi. Neither Allen Jerkens nor Bobby Frankel was involved.

"Who worries you?" I asked.

"That French horse, Rouvres, has got some class. He won a Grade I over there and he ran good a couple times at Saratoga, but I think we'll be all right. This may be the way we go from here on."

"Grass?"

"I'm thinking about it. Why should I go out to the Breeders' Cup Classic and tangle with Mineshaft again? The turf race should come up a lot easier."

He paused to cough and clear his throat.

"Put it this way," he said scratchily: "He wins the Classic again, that's the best of both worlds. But he runs it and loses, he'll always be remembered as the horse that couldn't repeat. If he wins the Turf, he'll be the only horse that ever won 'em both."

———

I watched the race on TVG. Volponi went off at 3-5 and broke well from the gate. Possibly too well, for Velazquez hurried him up the outside to contest the lead with State Shinto, the 6-1 third choice in the field of seven. After a gap of about three lengths, Rouvres, the 3-1 second choice, was third.

Nothing changed for the next half mile. Volponi stayed outside State Shinto, less than a length behind him, just as he'd run alongside Blue Boat at Saratoga.

Midway through the turn toward the homestretch, Velazquez made his move. To me, in front of the television set three thousand miles away, and on the basis of the twenty-five years in which I didn't watch a single horse race, it seemed a bit early to turn Volponi loose.

Velazquez, however, encountered none of the problems that Jerry Bailey had. Volponi took the lead smoothly and Velazquez guided him to the rail for the drive down the stretch. He opened a lead of two lengths, almost three.

"He's gonna win it! He's gonna win it!" I shouted to an empty room. "Volponi is finally gonna win another race!" And, with only three-sixteenths of a mile to go, it looked as if P.G.'s big horse not only would win, but would do so as impressively as he had eleven months earlier in the Classic.

Except he was not continuing to pull away. And instead of sinking like Blue Boat, State Shinto was hanging on. And suddenly both Rouvres and another horse, who'd come from farther back, were racing into contention.

Volponi still led by a head with an eighth of a mile to go. But Rouvres passed him, and then the other horse—Della Francesca, at 16-1—passed Rouvres.

And that's how they went under the wire. Much the fastest at the end, Della Francesca won by a length and a half, with Rouvres taking second from Volponi by a neck. Had I been only a spectator, with no special rooting interest, it would have been a hell of a horse race. Instead, it seemed a catastrophe.

After five straight second-place finishes, P.G. puts Volponi back on the grass, where he's the odds-on favorite, and he runs not even second, but third?! And tires in the final furlong of a mile-and-an-eighth turf race?! How would he ever get a mile and a quarter on the dirt?!

To have run a neck behind the consistent but never spectacular Rouvres was bad enough, but to be flown past by . . . what was his name?

Della Francesca. A horse partly owned by basketball coach Rick Pitino, and a horse whose only win since shipping over from Ireland the year before had been in an allowance race at Gulfstream in January.

It was one thing to run a courageous second to Mineshaft. It was one thing to lose to Medaglia d'Oro, with excuses. It might even have been one thing to get beat by an Allen Jerkens surprise after going wide and getting bumped.

But to have a perfect trip and run third to something called Della Francesca?

"He was going easy," Velazquez said after the race, "just galloping. I figured if I got after him on the turn, I could get away from everyone. He gave me a little acceleration, but not enough. It's not that he ever stopped running, he just never accelerated again."

I could only imagine how P.G.'s heart must have sunk. I waited until Monday before calling.

"It was good for my voice," he said. "I didn't have to hurt it cheering."

"What's next?"

"Jersey. I'm gonna do just like I did last year. I'll run him in that Meadowlands stakes at the start of October, and if he comes out of that good we'll be out to see you, and that'll be for the Classic, not the Turf. No more grass for him until he gets to the stud farm in Kentucky."

"Have you sold him?"

"Still workin' on it."

"I guess every time he loses you've got to drop the price a little more."

There was silence on the line. That was not an observation I'd needed to make. But at the rate of a million dollars off the sale price for every loss, Volponi had cost P.G. more in 2003 than he'd won for him in all the years before.

"Maybe I'll come see you first," I said. "How about for the Meadowlands race?"

"You know where to find me. Belmont, Barn Sixty-three. I'm there at four-thirty every morning."

2 I'd seen Rescigno the horse at Saratoga.

On my first morning at Belmont, I saw Rescigno.

Al Rescigno had been P.G.'s best friend in New York for forty years. That he'd also been one of mobster Joey Gallo's best friends for many years was not important—at least not to P.G.

"I met Al almost as soon as I got here," P.G. said.

Just by chance. I was walking out of Aqueduct one day—I think I'd had a horse paid a pretty big price—and he asked me when I was gonna have another. I wound up buying him a cup of coffee, we talked, we got along, and pretty soon he was bringing me some owners.

My understanding is he was probably Joey Gallo's best friend. They grew up together, went to school together, got thrown out of school together. I wouldn't say Al was one of Joey's gang, exactly, because he didn't do some of the things they did. But he was respected. And he was very close to Joey Gallo personally. And back then . . . well, let's just say I imagine that Al has some memories.

But the day his daughter was born—lovely girl, she's married now, kids of her own—he quit. He called up Joey and said, "No more. I don't know you anymore." Joey says, "Oh, come on, Al, we're friends. I never put you on a spot." But Al stuck to it. There was no bad feeling. Joey understood. Then, three or four years down the line, he got killed.

Al was in the catering business, in Brooklyn. He was doing catering for all the big guys. But he got into some trouble with the IRS. They took his house, his cars, he lost his business—he had nothing. He never went to prison, but they ruined him. Me, I don't give a shit what they say—I'll always be grateful to Al. He's been the best friend a man could have down through the years.

Rescigno the horse was a two-year-old with an injured leg and had never raced. Al Rescigno, at seventy-eight, was in terrific shape, even after two brain-tumor operations. He was a short, strong, barrel-chested man who moved with an athlete's quickness.

"I was a shortstop," he told me. "Then they wondered about my arm, so they moved me to second base. I was in the Chicago organization, Detroit, the Yankees. I spent one spring training with the Yankees. They put Frankie Crosetti and Phil Rizzuto in charge of me. Must've been thirty years later, I was at Madison Square Garden for a hockey game and Rizzuto walks by and makes a little gesture with his hand and gives me a smile and says, 'Rescigno.' He hadn't seen me in thirty years."

"What did you do?"

"I smiled back and went click with my hand and said, 'Rizzuto.' That was all."

Once cool, always cool: That was Al.

He bought me coffee and a bagel in the track kitchen, and as we rode back to the barn in his Cadillac we seemed on our way to friendship until I made the mistake of asking him what he thought of *The Sopranos.*

"That shit? You think I'd watch that shit? I don't know a fucking thing about *The Sopranos.* You'd have to be a real ass-hole to watch that show. Did you ever watch it?"

"All the time. I love it. I saw Michael Imperioli at Saratoga this summer. Looked just like he looks on the show. You know, Christopher, Tony's cousin?"

"I don't want to hear nothin' about the fuckin' *Sopranos,*" Al said. And when I went to the races with P.G. that afternoon, Al sat elsewhere.

———

The real shock wasn't so much P.G.'s voice (though it had worsened discernibly since Saratoga), it was his sunglasses.

"What's this?" I said. "You in training for L.A.?" Even at my age, I still said dumb things.

"I got cataracts. I'm gonna have to have 'em removed once I get done with a few more tests about my throat. My throat, they say now one of the vocal cords is paralyzed. That ain't good. My eyes, the doctor said I've gotta wear the shades whenever I'm outside in the daylight."

"It's not a bad look, actually. In fact, they make you look like a friend of Al Rescigno's."

"Well, they make me feel like a blind man. If I bring a tin cup to the paddock, maybe some rich owner will drop a dime in."

———

For someone without cataracts, Belmont was beautiful in early October: brilliant blue sky, strong sun, light breeze, temperature in the upper 50s. It also was empty.

I had not been to Belmont since the day Seattle Slew clinched his Triple Crown there in 1977. Attendance that day had been more than 70,000. On the afternoon of Friday, October 3, 2003, attendance was 3,761.

In 1977, of course, there had been a Triple Crown at stake and it had been a Saturday. And even in 2003, in a downpour, Funny Cide's try for the Triple Crown had drawn the biggest crowd in Belmont history. That wasn't the point. What struck me was how, in the absence of a highly promoted, heavily advertised special event, or an eBay-able giveaway such as a bobblehead, people simply did not go to the races anymore.

Bizarrely, this almost seemed the way that those at the top of the pyramid preferred it: Lower attendance meant fewer forced interactions with the great unwashed. It was an inbred, closed (and still flagrantly anti-Semitic) society, this highest echelon of Thoroughbred racing: dominated by myopically self-absorbed white, Anglo-Saxon Protestants, many of whom had achieved precious little on their own, but who seemed to believe that their ancestors' success in systematically and cynically pillaging the American free-enterprise system entitled them to be treated like nineteenth-century European royalty, even in post-9/11 New York.

In any event, of the 3,761 souls who had blown in on the Belmont breeze that Friday, I would have laid odds that three-quarters of them were housed in bodies that had been on earth longer than my own. Horse racing in America truly seemed a dying sport, of interest only to dying old men.

Belmont, of course, was not uppermost on P.G.'s mind that afternoon. Across the Hudson, shortly after 10 P.M., Volponi would go off as the heavy favorite in a six-horse field in the $400,000 Grade II Meadowlands Breeders' Cup Stakes. At Belmont, on Friday, P.G. was just punching the clock.

Micmaceuse, the filly who'd kept his Saratoga streak alive—the filly who'd made me rich in my dreams—finished last among ten in the first race, preceded only slightly by stablemate Ellie's Quest. After One Tough Dude ran third in the second race, we went back to the barn for the serious work, which was the vanning of Volponi to New Jersey.

Except for P.G. slipping and almost falling on the ramp (the sunglasses crimped his peripheral vision), the process went smoothly. Ocala would ride with the driver, and a groom would stay in the rear of the van with the horse. At age five, Volponi was a seasoned traveler, bothered far less by either airplane or van than by the starting gate.

The slightly more tenuous travel arrangement involved jockey Velazquez, who'd flown to Keeneland that morning to ride a horse of Todd Pletcher's in a $400,000 stakes race. The Kentucky race would go off at 5:15, which, given clear skies, would allow Velazquez to fly by private plane to New Jersey in plenty of time for Volponi. As a contingency, P.G. had arranged for Shaun Bridgmohan—one of the horse's previous riders, and a young jockey in whom he had confidence—to stand by.

"I guess you'll be going home to change," I said, once Volponi's van had pulled out.

"Into pajamas."

"You've got time for a nap? Well, I guess since the race isn't until ten."

"By which time I'll be sound asleep."

"What?"

"Hell, I'm not *going* to the race. Have you ever been to the Meadowlands? It's miserable over there, especially at night. The wind blows, you freeze your ass off, the traffic coming back is impossible. Shit, I haven't been to the Meadowlands in ten years."

"But this is Volponi!"

"So? You think he'll know I'm not there? Don't worry, I'll come with him to California, but I'm too goddamned old to go to Jersey. If you want to go, you can go. Kathy and Karen and them will be in the clubhouse dining room; you'll be able to find them. But I'm going home for dinner and I'm going to bed."

"You're going to be able to sleep while Volponi is running his last prep for the Breeders' Cup Classic?"

"I did last year. I told Mary Kay only to wake me if he won. He was second. I slept like a log."

"But you're his trainer. You're his breeder. You're his *owner*! He's your big horse!"

"Ed will be there, my partner. My daughters will be there. My granddaughter will be there. You can be there if you want. But as long as Ocala's with him, I know he's fine. And now I'm gonna get the hell out of this barn before I cough my lungs out."

I didn't know what to do. Among his many other distinctions, P.G. was the all-time leading stakes-winning trainer in the history of the Meadowlands, but even with the first big horse of his life running his last prep race before the Breeders' Cup Classic, P.G. was going home to bed.

He was right, of course: The Meadowlands (beneath which Jimmy Hoffa's body supposedly was buried, something I thought I wouldn't ask Al Rescigno about) was as unappealing as racetracks got. And driving to New Jersey from Long Island during rush hour at the start of a weekend would be almost as gruesome as driving in Southern California. But the race would be on neither television nor radio. Nor, given the state of horse racing in modern America, was the result likely even to be broadcast on the 11 P.M. news.

P.G. must have detected my unease.

"Give me your cell phone number," he said. "And make sure you got juice in it. I'll have one of the kids call you from the track before the race. Turn up the volume and maybe you can even hear the call. And don't look so heartbroken. You can see the horse at five o'clock tomorrow morning."

———

I spent the night in my hotel room, paging through some of P.G.'s scrapbooks. Karen's husband, Noel Michaels, who also worked at the *Daily Racing Form,* called me just before 10 P.M.

"Everything's fine," he said. "Velazquez got here. We're

just going down to the paddock. How about if I call you back as soon as it's over."

"Okay. How's the betting?"

"He's 4-5. Dynever is the only other horse getting money."

I knew Dynever. He was an improving three-year-old of considerable quality, trained by Christophe Clement, who also trained Rouvres and had the barn next to P.G. at Saratoga. Corey Nakatani had flown all the way from California to ride him. I was afraid of Dynever.

"When's post time?"

"10:24."

"Okay, so you can call about 10:26?"

"As soon as it's official."

"I'll be here."

I put down the phone and waited.

10:24.

10:25.

10:26.

What the hell?

10:27.

10:28.

Okay, he won. Obviously, he won, and Noel and the others were rushing down to the winner's circle. That's all it could be. That's what it had to be.

10:29.

No news is good news. No news is good news.

10:30.

10:31.

What the *fuck*?!

The phone rang.

I grabbed it.

"He was third."

"*What?*"

"Actually, he finished fourth, but got moved up to third on a disqualification."

"*What?*"

"He got pinched back between horses at the start, and then he was never really in it. He was beaten five lengths, I guess. Bowman's Band won it. Dynever was second."

"*Who* won it?"

"Bowman's Band. That's a horse Allen Jerkens took over just this week. He paid twenty-six sixty. Amazing, isn't it? Jerkens did it again. Listen, I've got to go. There's some pretty disappointed people around here right now."

———

I didn't get to the barn until six. I figured P.G. needed some time alone with his horse.

"We almost lost him," he said. "Excuse me, but is that coffee?"

"Yeah. Do you want some?"

"You'll have to take that outside. I'm sorry. No coffee allowed in the barn."

For me, it was still very early. I wasn't sure I was tracking. Was this a joke?

"Somebody should have told you," he said. "I should have told you. No coffee, no tea, no cola in the barn. What happens is people have those little styrofoam cups, and when they're finished, they drop it in the nearest bucket, which is usually a feed tub. They don't think about it, of course, but ten drops of black coffee, or half an ounce of Coke in the food, and a horse will test positive for stimulant. I got enough fucking problems without people juicing my horses by accident."

Live and learn. I took my coffee outside and dumped it. But I still wasn't sure what he had said first.

"A quarter inch," he said, when I stepped back inside. "The horse outside him slammed into him as soon as they broke from the gate and knocked him into the horse on the inside. One of them sliced the inside of his ankle with a shoe, or he did it himself when he got smacked. It's not a bad cut, if we can keep it from getting infected, but it's only a quarter inch from the main blood vessel in the foot."

"A quarter inch?"

"Like this." He held up a thumb and forefinger, almost touching. "He wouldn't have bled to death, but he sure as hell wouldn't have raced again this year, which means he wouldn't ever have raced again. When it gets lighter, I'll take you down to his stall and show you. And I'll show you the head-on videotape: You'll see him get slammed and squeezed as soon as they break. Like the Whitney, the fuckin' race was over for me as soon as it started, but this was worse. The goddamned horse was almost over, too."

"What did Velazquez say?"

"Let's not talk about Velazquez. He must have fallen asleep on his airplane from Kentucky and not woke up. The son of a bitch didn't even claim foul. It was the stewards who made the inquiry and moved me up. And do you know why he didn't claim foul? Because he thought he was third. He didn't realize he was fourth. He told Cordero he thought he'd finished third. Can you believe that? The leading jockey in New York, and he can't tell if he finishes third or fourth? You see why I call them all pinheads? Go drink a cup of coffee. I'm not goin' anywhere. I'll show you the head-on when you get back."

As I started out the door, he called after me. "Now you know why I don't go to Jersey."

It was a tense morning at the barn. A vet came to medicate and rebandage Volponi's foot. Half owner Ed Baier, who had been at the Meadowlands, arrived. He looked as if he had not slept.

"Got an hour or two," he said. "There was a lane closed on the Cross-Bronx coming back and it took four and a half hours to get home. I'm the luckiest guy who ever bought half a horse, but I think I hear the fat lady starting to sing."

P.G. called Nan Miller, the acupuncturist and chiropractor, to arrange a Monday morning evaluation and treatment for Volponi. "That horse," he said, "will never want to see a starting gate again. Used to be he just didn't like bein' in 'em. Now, he gets mugged when he comes out."

"You could send him to Europe," I said. "Those races where they don't use starting gates. They just all stand around behind a wire."

"Where I'm gonna send him," P.G. said, "is to Kentucky, where he can forget all about starting gates and learn what a breeding shed is. But I'll be goddamned if he's goin' out on this note. You know Al Jolson's my favorite singer. Now it's just like the Al Jolson song."

" 'Mammy'?" Ed Baier said.

" 'Swanee'?" I said.

"Wake up, for Christ's sake: 'California, Here I Come.' "

————

Saturday was a big day at Belmont. Or would have been if Belmont still had big days other than the occasional Belmont Stakes Day with a Triple Crown up for grabs.

It was the day of the Champagne Stakes, a premier fall event for two-year-olds. And the Champagne was only one of four stakes races on the card, three of them Grade I. It would be preceded by the Frizette, a $500,000 Grade I for two-year-old fillies, and followed by both the Kelso Handicap, a $350,000 Grade II run at one mile on the turf, and by the afternoon's biggest race, the $750,000 Grade I Beldame at a mile and an eighth, a race that would match Bobby Frankel's Sightseek against Barclay Tagg's Island Fashion and Allen Jerkens's Passing Shot, among others.

It was a racing program of stunning quality. There had been four stakes on the Travers Day card at Saratoga that had drawn a crowd of more than 60,000, but only two had been Grade I, and total purse money had been $1.6 million, compared to the $2.1 million offered for Belmont's four stakes.

The Champagne alone, in which the best two-year-olds in the East run farther than seven furlongs for the first time in their lives, is a fixture with a dazzling history. I vividly remembered attending in 1969, as Sonny Werblin's Silent Screen, ridden by John L. Rotz, held off Brave Emperor—and the jockey who would always be my favorite, because he'd won my first Kentucky Derby for me, Braulio Baeza—through the stretch, to win by a length.

Because the New York Mets were playing a World Series game against the Baltimore Orioles the same afternoon, the race drew only about 35,000 to Belmont, the lowest Saturday attendance of the fall season.

Forgetting again that that was then and this was now, I made sure to reach the track more than an hour before the 1 P.M. post time for the first race. The place was so empty I could have parked on the finish line. It was eerie. I rode the escalator from level to level, but found only clusters of bedraggled old men, smoking cigarettes, scribbling marks on the pages of their racing papers, or staring blankly into the distance with rheumy eyes. It was like being, not in a place where people came to have fun, but in the recreation room of a nursing home.

And this was Belmont Park on a Saturday in October with four stakes races on the card, including the Champagne and the Beldame. There was neither a World Series nor a National Football League game nor any other competing sporting event to lure spectators elsewhere. It was simply that nobody cared anymore.

There had not been a word in the morning's *New York Times* about the extraordinary day of racing that was about to unfold, nor even about the $400,000 race at the Meadowlands the night before. Horse racing no longer existed as a mainstream spectator sport in America. The dog show got more respect.

P.G.'s role on Champagne Day was brief and inconsequential. The day was so darkly overcast that he cheated and took off his sunglasses. The way his horses ran, he would have been better off blindfolded.

In the first race, Volponi's unmotivated and underachieving younger half brother, Gentle Nudge—the most nonchalant of all the horses in P.G.'s barn—enjoyed another fresh-air frolic at 30-1, cantering around the track well to the rear of most of his brethren, as if auditioning for a job as stable pony.

An hour later, the entry of Lex and Sully's Silver ran fifth and seventh, at 11-1. P.G. said he was going home to watch the big races on television. Certainly, there was nothing in the cheerless ambience of the clubhouse that would make a man want to stay. Attendance was later announced as 7,591. There were more cars than that in the parking lot of the nearest Wal-Mart.

Allen Jerkens's Society Selection won the Frizette in an upset. Coming on the heels of Bowman's Band's win over Dynever and Volponi at the Meadowlands, it gave Jerkens two long-shot stakes wins at two different tracks within eighteen hours. *Plus ça change,* as I would have said if I spoke French. The old Giant Killer was becoming a megatrainer at last.

Jerry Bailey won the Champagne on Nick Zito's impressive Birdstone while a 20-1 shot called Freefourinternet won the Kelso Handicap. Rouvres was third. Then Bailey came back aboard Bobby Frankel's Sightseek at 3-10 to win the Beldame by five lengths.

Frankel's slump was over. I had my doubts about P.G.'s, but I was more worried about his health than his slump. His energy seemed to have ebbed since Saratoga, and his voice had deteriorated even further.

It did not help, of course, that Volponi had lost twice more since leaving Saratoga, and had come within a hair's breadth of a career-ending injury.

Nor was it comforting that even at an asking price of $3 million—less than one-third of the price that had been anticipated at the start of the year—the list of prospective buyers for Volponi had few names on it.

Nor could it have cheered P.G. to see how execrably most of his other horses were running. He'd had only a single win in a maiden race to show for nineteen starts at Belmont, and most of his entrants had wound up closer to last than to first.

The deepening chill in his barn seemed to emanate from something even beyond the frosty predawn temperatures of October. Perhaps it was his sense—not that this was something I was eager to discuss with him—that there might be only one horse standing between him and the probable end of sixty years of doing what he loved.

And even that horse now was standing none too comfortably in his stall.

Monday morning was cold enough for hats and gloves, and for the first time since moving to California I had to scrape ice off the windshield of my car.

"I guess Florida looks better every day," I said.

"It looks great, but this is as close to it as I'm gonna get."

"What, you're not going down?"

"I can't. These cataracts, I gotta get them taken out. And I don't know what else is happening. This crap with my voice. I've had some new tests. I told you about the paralyzed vocal cord. They don't like some other things, either. So they gotta do more tests. I've got some goddamned MRI thing this afternoon. There might be some kind of growth in there that didn't used to be there the last time they checked. If that's the case, it'll have to come out. Some kind of polyp or something."

"When would that happen?"

"After California. See, that's what I'm faced with: If I wind up in some goddamned hospital for an operation in November, and then I got the cataracts, and then there's the holidays—by the time I was ready to go to Florida it would be time to come back."

"I guess Mary Kay's happy, at least. She didn't want you to go."

"I'm going to tell you something. Mary Kay is not happy. Mary Kay is not accepting aging well. There's a block there. 'Oh, you're going to be this, I'm going to be that, we're going to be like this and that, and it will be awful.' I says, 'So what? Most guys my age couldn't get on the treadmill, let alone plug it in and turn it on.' I said, 'I didn't give myself prostate cancer. And we got over that. We got lucky, we got the right doctors. And we'll get 'em again if we need 'em.' "

But now, instead of having Florida on the horizon, P.G. was facing another cold winter in New York.

———

It was time to change Volponi's dressing.

Crouching, and with my back to the wall, I followed P.G. and Ocala into the stall.

"You go slow," Ocala said. "He no like company in his home."

He was a beautiful animal. He was also immense, high-strung, in at least some pain, and scary as hell to step behind. But I maneuvered into the spot where P.G. wanted me to be, and I crouched down to look at the inside of his ankle, where he'd been cut.

"It's healing nice. He'll be fine. But look at this." P.G. put his hand around the ankle and pressed a spot just above the slice.

"How I knew it was the blood vessel," he said, "I put my finger on the vessel right above it, and this little scrape turned bright red. That's the artery. A quarter inch, maybe even less. If that had got nicked, he'd still be gettin' transfusions."

We stood. "You gotta be lucky," P.G. said. "No matter how fuckin' brilliant you think you are, you gotta be lucky, or you're dead. Now, I gotta go call the pinhead's agent."

"Which pinhead?"

"The pinniest pinhead of all. The pinhead of pinheads: Santos."

"How come?"

"Because I'm puttin' him back on the horse."

———

P.G. and Mary Kay and I ate dinner at a small Italian restaurant in Rockville Centre. He started with a Grey Goose martini, straight up.

"I don't really want it tonight," he said, "but I can't come in here no more without havin' Grey Goose."

"How come?"

"Because he made a fool of himself about them not having it a few months ago, that's how come," Mary Kay said.

"I didn't make a fool of myself. I made a point. Back in the spring, before Saratoga, we come in here and I order Grey Goose and they say they don't have it anymore. 'Why not?' Because it's French, and they want to prove how goddamned patriotic American they are—bunch of Italians, right?—by not carrying anything from France. Well, I got the manager over here, and we got into it pretty good. He says Iraq this and Iraq that and Bush this and Bush that, and France isn't supporting us, and I said, 'Just a goddamn minute. Whose side were you on in the real war?' 'The real war?' 'Yeah, World War goddamned Two. I happened to be in that war. And one of the things that kept me awake at night was I had to be afraid that my goddamned ship was going to get blown out of the ocean by you Italians, who had signed up with the Nazis. And now I come in here and you tell me that you're an American patriot because you won't let me drink the brand of vodka I want? That's not being a patriot, that's being an asshole.' "

"I was mortified," Mary Kay said. "I thought they were going to call the police."

"What did they do?"

"They sent a busboy out," P.G. said, "and he ran down to that liquor store around the corner, and he came back with a bottle of Grey Goose, and I got my martini. But now I've gotta have one every time."

Once he'd had his martini—and I'd had mine—I asked what on earth had made him decide to use Jose Santos on Volponi again.

"I've looked at that Meadowlands race fifty times.

Velazquez just doesn't have a feel for this horse. You can't try to force him to do something, because he's not gonna be intimidated. John got panicky about being pinched back, and so going into the turn he's like cowboys and Indians all of a sudden, whoopin' and hollerin' and waving his arms and his whip, and the horse finally says, 'If that's how you're gonna be, forget it.'

"Remember what I told you about Cordero getting busy gradually? And about why trainers take jockeys off horses? This is an example of that. Velazquez is obviously a capable rider, and he's also a decent kid. He's married to Leo O'Brien's daughter, and Leo's one of the smartest trainers around and one of the best guys in the business. But every rider doesn't suit every horse.

"The great ones—the very greatest, like Steve Cauthen and Shoemaker, and I'll put Cordero in that company, and maybe one or two others in my whole life—they can get the best out of almost any horse. But then you go to the fifty or so excellent riders, and in that group some match up with certain horses better than others.

"Listen, I'll say it straight, although I can't say it to the press because I'd be knockin' a guy who just won sixty-one fuckin' races at Saratoga, but it was the rider who got beat at the Meadowlands, not the horse. Santos did give me a lousy ride in the Whitney, but he knows the horse better than anyone, and he especially knows the horse at a mile and a quarter. Besides, he's the last guy to win a race on him. And this'll be Volponi's last race, so why not put the team back together?"

"You sure this is really your idea?" I said.

"Of course it is. Who else's would it be?"

"I don't know. It's almost too dramatic. I thought maybe the guys from Disney."

"Shit, they wanted me to ride him myself."

———

I got to the barn before the sun rose on Tuesday morning. Volponi was being readied for his first exposure to the track since the Meadowlands. P.G.'s top exercise rider, an experienced Chilean named Mario, was in the saddle. P.G. drove to the apron of the grandstand near the head of the Belmont homestretch.

Fog lay close to the ground. The temperature was in the upper 30s. "See, jogging, if he's lame from any of his problems, he'll nod his head up and down as he moves. So, look for that when we see him jog up to the quarter pole here. If he's okay, Mario will give me a nod, then we'll gallop him around to about the three-quarter pole over there in the backstretch. It's funny with soreness. You can tell it in the front end better with the jogging, but the back end you see better when they gallop, because they give these little bunny hops, you know how a bunny puts his feet down together?"

Behind the spacious Belmont infield, the sun began to rise. I'd been coming to Belmont since the late 1950s, but I'd never before seen the sun rise over the infield. I'd also never before sat in a car at the quarter pole with a Hall of Fame trainer whose first and only big horse was in the final phases of preparation for the last race of his life—a race with a $4 million purse.

"Here he comes," P.G. said. His gaze was rapt.

"All right, all right," he whispered.

Mario spotted P.G.'s car and nodded.

"Okay, turn him around," P.G. called, making a circular motion with his arm. Volponi turned and moved from a jog to a slow gallop.

"See how smooth he's goin'? That's thanks to Nan. She unkinked him, and we'll do it again before we ship. Now see further down? That's One Tough Dude. He ran good the other day. Excuse me, he ran well. I could never work for Wayne Lukas. He says you gotta have good grammar to be in his barn." P.G. put his car in gear and started back to the barn.

"You probably wouldn't want to work for Lukas anyway."

"I don't think I'd do him any good."

"Has he ever done you any good?"

"No, he hasn't. He doesn't bother me anymore—hell,

these days he's just another senior citizen. But in his heyday he was bad."

"Bad how?"

"I said I never had a rich owner. I had one. Edward Evans. I had Dance Teacher for him, won a Grade I stakes with her at Aqueduct, mile and a quarter, in November. She won hands down, just galloping. A week later I sent her and two other fillies he owned to his farm in Virginia. I kept one with me. I was gonna race 'em all again in the spring.

"Then Evans went to California, and I started to hear things. One day, he went to Santa Anita, naturally to the Trustees' Room, and he met Lukas. And they got together pretty good. I didn't hear a word of this from Evans, by the way. He was a gentleman, I'll say that. Still is. I'm still very friendly with him; I talk to him all the time.

"But Lukas nailed him for Dance Teacher, my Grade I winner. Next thing I hear, she's gone to California. All of a sudden, she's Lukas's horse, not mine. Then Evans's farm manager calls from Virginia and says he's sending the other two fillies back to me.

"I said, 'Let me ask you a question, and allow me to answer it. Dance Teacher went to Lukas in California, right?' And he says, 'Yes.' I said, 'Well, you send those other two fillies to Lukas, too. And you tell Lukas to come get this son of a bitch I have here as quick as he can.' And Lukas sent, I don't remember who it was, it might have been Pletcher, one of his assistants, and took that horse, and that was the end of it.

"You win a Grade I race with a horse that you work all summer and talk the guy into running on the dirt . . . That's the thing about rich owners: They screw you. They screw *you*. Dance Teacher, a Grade I winner. And you know what? She never ran again. I don't know what the hell happened, but he fired Lukas within three months."

We reached the barn and stood outside, waiting for Volponi to return. The sun was up now, and P.G. put on his sunglasses. "Here's the big guy," he said. "Was he okay, Mario?"

The rider smiled and gave a thumbs-up.

"Good deal," P.G. said, smiling. "Yup, he's all right. Dodged a bullet. Quarter of an inch. I don't care how smart you are, you gotta be lucky."

Phil and Mary Kay Johnson

3 There was no racing at Belmont on Mondays and Tues-days, so on Tuesday afternoon I visited P.G. and Mary Kay at their home in Rockville Centre. It was a lovely house on a quiet street in a fine old neighborhood. They'd been living there for thirty years.

The original of a "PEB" sketch of P.G. from the 1970s hung on one wall. He had long, curly hair and large, horn-rimmed glasses, and there was a cigar in his mouth. Given a hundred guesses, I would never have thought it was P.G.

"Might be time for a new caricature," I said.

"I'd hate to see what he'd do to me now."

"You'd have nothing to worry about. He's almost as old as you are."

"But he don't look it."

"That's because he's got a young Haitian wife, and she keeps him on a very strict regimen."

"There you go, Phil," Mary Kay said. "That's what you ought to do."

"Which one? The strict regimen or the young Haitian wife?"

"What's your preference?" Mary Kay said.

"Maybe a strict wife and a Haitian regimen," he said.

"So you don't think you've already got the strict wife?" she said.

"Oh, you're not so bad, except you never let me spend any money."

"If I let you spend what you wanted to spend, we'd be living in the barn with your horses."

"You know why Mary Kay was happy about our girls growing up? Because when they were kids I used to go to that big toy store across from the Plaza hotel in New York City—FAO Schwarz, it was called—and I'd have a cup of tea in the Plaza, and then I'd go to the toy store and I'd turn into a little kid again, and I'd come home with one of practically everything. There was nothin' I ever wanted bad enough to go out and spend money on myself, but I did go a little overboard with the kids."

"I understand Schwarz is going out of business, or filed for bankruptcy, or something," I said.

"Well, you see," Mary Kay said. "It was only Phil keeping them going."

"He's not as bad as Wayne Lukas," I said. "I was just reading where a bunch of Lukas's friends a few years ago had to have an intervention, like they do for drug addicts or alcoholics, and they all confronted him about how he kept throwing his money away and wound up so much in debt."

"I don't know about that," P.G. said, "but he sure had a lot of ways of making it. I'll tell you a story about him. You know, I mentioned this one owner I had, Howard Kaskel, really a very sweet guy. He wanted me to come down to Keeneland with him to buy something at the Fasig-Tipton [auction company] sale. So, we're down there and I had marked a filly I thought we should maybe buy. I go over to him, and he's sitting there with all these New York geniuses— real estate guys and politicians—and he says, 'Oh, no, Wayne Lukas says she's no good at all.'

"Now I knew the consigner, Charley Knuckles, one of those guys. Straight arrow, no-nonsense guy. So I went back around and I looked at her again. They brought the filly out. I'd already looked at her once. I said, 'Have you had a lot of lookers?' He said, 'No, not really.' I said, 'Did Wayne Lukas look at her?' He said, 'Yes, he did.' I said, 'Evidently he didn't like her.' He said, 'Oh, he liked her.' 'Well, he told my owner he didn't, but I do, and I want to buy her for my owner, so tell me why he didn't like her.'

"He says, 'I'm gonna tell you something, Johnson. He asked me what I thought she'd bring, and I said around fifty-sixty thousand. Lukas says, "What if she brings a hundred and twenty-five? What do I get out of it?" And I said you get nothing out of it. Get the fuck away from here.'

"Okay. That was all I wanted to know. That was Lukas.

And the filly? She won the two-year-old filly stake at Churchill Downs on Derby Day the following spring.

"I'm not knocking what Lukas did. I never did that stuff myself, but a lot of guys figure when there's so much money multiplied by so much stupidity—which is what you got with a lot of owners, like they're walkin' around with a sign on that says 'Screw Me'—well, it's like a license to take advantage.

"And I can tell you one thing Lukas figured out, which is what I had known for years: You train ordinary horses for so much per day and 10 percent, you're gonna be out of the business. Or, worse, you're gonna owe so much money that the bad guys will keep you in the business, hoping you get lucky so you can pay them.

"Here's how you can tell how tough it is to make it as a trainer if you only got other people's horses and you're honest. Look at how many trainers quit to become jockeys' agents. There's very few worse jobs in racing than being a jockey's agent, which is not a knock against the people that do it, because some of them are good people, but you've seen all the scurrying around that's involved, and what do they get? Ten percent of their rider's 10 percent. But even so—even so—a lot of hardworking and capable trainers have quit because you got a better shot at making enough to eat on as a jockey's agent than you do with a barn full of somebody else's horses at seventy-five bucks a day.

"I respect the training profession. I've been in it all my life and I respect it, and I have great respect for most of the people in it. I know some guys get down on their luck and they've gotta cheat and they've gotta steal, and they do terrible things, but I understand. When you got a couple of kids at home, you do things. How I avoided that, and managed to keep my self-respect, is I started to breed my own horses. That's what got us above the poverty level. You cannot do it simply as a trainer with a public stable anymore."

"I hate to say it," Mary Kay said, "but we're a dying breed. When we look back on all the people, there's not that many left but Allen and Phil. The others are retired or gone. For anyone who was around in the old days, there's a sadness."

"In the old days," P.G. said, "we would socialize in Florida with Sonny Hine and his wife, with Angel Penna. Angel died. The other guy's dead."

"And Mack and Martha we were very social with."

"Mack Miller. He retired."

"Outside of Tommy Trotter—he was the racing secretary here for so long, but even before that he was our dearest friend from Chicago—I'd say the best friend I had, and still have, is Lucille Stephens, Woody's wife," Mary Kay said.

"But she's in Florida," P.G. said. "Doesn't travel much."

"We're not standoffish," Mary Kay said.

"Well, we went to dinner with the Derby-winner trainer," P.G. said, "but he's the only trainer we've been to dinner with this year, except John Hertler, and John's like family. He used to work for me before Ocala. You see, the younger guys, they're different: Some of them are using a lot of cocaine and marijuana. Which I'm not saying they shouldn't—that's their business, and God knows some of the old-timers drank enough to kill their horses as well as themselves—but that's not an atmosphere I socialize in."

"We're open to go to dinner with anybody," Mary Kay said. "But I wouldn't know who to ask."

"Nobody's asking you?" I said.

"No," P.G. said.

"Oh, no. No, no, no, no, no," Mary Kay said.

"You've gotten to be too revered," I said.

He laughed. "Oh, no."

"You know what he's gotten to be?" Mary Kay said. "Too old."

"I beg your pardon," P.G. said.

"Oh, come on, face it." She turned to me. "You know what we did, almost every Sunday of our life, we went to Bethpage, here on the island, to the polo, because Allen Jerkens always played. And then we would go to Allen's house, and Annie, his wife, would have a table—this long, long table—set for about thirty people, and she put on the food like you would not believe. You know, it wasn't fancy, but it was wonderful, and there were all the other racetrackers there."

"But what happened," P.G. said, "I used to go to dinner with him sometimes. Or we'd go for lunch if we didn't have a horse in. Or I'd go over when he fed his horses in the afternoon. And we would talk while he walked around the barn, because he would really only talk to other trainers. You gotta know him damn well to talk. But I could say anything to him."

"And you do," Mary Kay said.

"I do. When we're alone. 'You really screwed that one up, Allen. I'm not proud of you anymore. The jockeys you ride, you're lucky they don't fall off.' Now, don't let any stranger try to say that to him. But then, when he got this other woman, which is his business—she became his wife after Annie died—she would pop up whenever anybody would encounter him at the barn. She would appear. And she would walk around with us, while he was checking the tubs and looking at the horses. And all at once he would never say anything in front of her. Pretty soon, I knew that's not the place for me anymore, so I stopped going. And a couple guys told me—Rick Violette, he's a hell of a good horseman, and a fine guy, too, he used to go around with him, and he said, 'I can't do that anymore.' It wasn't that anybody disliked her, but what had been special times with Allen, you just couldn't have them anymore."

"You see, Annie died of cancer," Mary Kay said. "And everybody loved her. And I think a lot of us older wives, well, we just didn't like the way Liz seemed to move in and take over Allen's life."

"Elisabeth," P.G. said.

"Oh, that's right," Mary Kay said. "I started to call her 'Liz,' once, and she told me, 'I prefer to be addressed as Elisabeth.' And once she got mad at Phil because he was at Allen's barn, and he picked up a cup to drink a cup of coffee, and she came in and yelled at him because he had picked up the cup that said 'Chief.' That was apparently Allen's cup, and no one else was supposed to touch it."

"So," P.G. said, "we can't go to dinner with Allen anymore. It would be too uncomfortable for all of us. He's the finest trainer I've ever known, and probably the finest man I've ever known in racing, and I'll always consider him my closest friend on the track, but for the four of us—it's just not possible. But I don't want to talk anymore about that."

"Less and less is possible, Phil," Mary Kay said.

"Next, she'll tell you she hates getting old," he said.

"Well, I do. And so do you, you're just too stubborn to admit it."

"Why waste time hating something you can't do anything about? Besides, there's always gonna be the new two-year-olds in the spring."

The afternoon light was waning. I said good-bye. I told P.G. and Mary Kay that I was looking forward to seeing them, and Volponi, in California.

"We'll be there," P.G. rasped. "Don't doubt that."

"And, believe it or not, we were young once," Mary Kay said. "Don't doubt *that*."

3 Santa Anita

1 The Breeders' Cup had been around for twenty years, but outside the game, or sport, or business, or industry of horse racing, it had never elicited much more than yawns.

At the start, it must have seemed a splendid idea: a single day of racing—at a different showpiece track each year—that would determine world champions in each of seven different divisions. And television became an enthusiastic partner, with NBC broadcasting a four-hour program that included live coverage of each race.

The public, however, voted with its remote. By 2000, audience share had dropped from 13 to 5 percent, and the rating from 5.1 to 1.7, putting the Breeders' Cup about on a par with Major League Soccer.

This failure arose from a fatal conceptual flaw: the failure to recognize that the public can whip itself into a frenzy for a single horse race once a year, but that seven "championship" events in one afternoon are six too many.

Moreover, the Kentucky Derby, the only horse race in the world ever to have achieved mythic status, is held on the first Saturday in May, in a section of the country redolent with the richness and promise of spring. It evokes the fragile, winsome ambience of Stephen Foster, and salutes the perennial promise of youth, as fresh young horses are asked to extend themselves over a greater distance than any at which they've ever been tested before. Derby Day draws participants and spectators alike into a fabulous fantasy world—all merry, all happy and bright—and assures them that at least one dream will come true.

The Breeders' Cup, by contrast, is the culmination of a yearlong war of attrition. It is *Survivor,* as opposed to the Derby's *American Idol.* In addition, its ever-changing location gives it more the aura of a floating crap game than national sporting event. Within the industry, a growing number of horsemen have come to view it as a Frankenstein monster, wreaking havoc with sensible training programs, and overshadowing dozens of traditional stakes races around which many tracks had formerly constructed their fall calendars.

Moreover, the very Kentucky breeders who had conceived the event as a means of boosting their prestige—and net worth—are bailing out. Hence the unseemly spectacle of U.S. Ambassador to England William Farish, a founding member of the Breeders' Cup board of directors, opting to retire the four-year-old Mineshaft to stud rather than risk a loss in the Classic that might diminish his initial value as a stallion.

"There's a lot of people involved that come into play

now," Mineshaft's trainer, Neil Howard, said. "The breeding industry, that's where it all starts."

And where it all ends, too. The tail, in other words, is wagging the horse. Instead of being bred to race, the Thoroughbreds of the twenty-first century are raced—sparingly and selectively—primarily to boost their value to the breeding industry. And it has become clear that *industry*, not *sport*, is the operative word.

As Jay Hovdey wrote in the *Daily Racing Form*, The Breeders' Cup, once the pot of gold at the end of the season's rainbow, suddenly has become a negative force field, a scary place from which to run screaming into the night. . . . Thoroughbreds, more than ever, have become as frail as hothouse flowers, liable to go as bad as runny cheese with barely a hard race, or exposure to harsh language.

Indeed, in the days leading up to the October 25 race, it was starting to look as if Volponi might win the Classic by default. Not only was Mineshaft out, but Juddmonte Farms (aka Khalid Abdullah) elected to cut short the career of Empire Maker, opting to rush the three-year-old Belmont Stakes winner to the breeding shed, where his $100,000 stud fee would equal Mineshaft's. Then the undefeated Argentinian-bred four-year-old, Candy Ride, who had beaten Medaglia d'Oro at Del Mar, was declared out because—or so I read—his feet were too small.

Running counter to the trend, and notwithstanding the effect on Barclay Tagg's blood pressure, Funny Cide's owners announced that, despite his eighty-seven-day layoff, their colt *would* run in the Classic. "He might as well get beat there as anywhere else," Tagg said, proving again that he wasn't inhaling from the same helium tank as his employers.

P.G. felt sorry for his friend Barclay, but not so sorry that he let Jose Santos jump from Volponi to Funny Cide when Barclay asked him to. "To tell you the truth, he doesn't want to switch," P.G. told me, "but I've agreed to play bad guy so the owners don't think he's disloyal. That way he can stay on the horse next year."

Deprived of Santos's services, Tagg opted for America's best and favorite female rider, the California-based, squeaky-voiced (and even with his own voice failing so badly, P.G. still managed a splendid imitation) Julie Krone.

"A Classic victory by Funny Cide would be a tearjerker on a scale of Seabiscuit's rally from the clouds in this summer's blockbuster movie," Steven Crist wrote in the *Daily Racing Form*. "The added attraction of Julie Krone's riding the gelding for the first time makes it so sweet a story that your teeth hurt just thinking about it."

But Crist, ever the realist, thought such an outcome "about as likely as a snowstorm at Santa Anita." He wrote:

History and basic handicapping suggest that Funny Cide is a much better bet to finish last than first in the Classic. . . . Funny Cide has not raced since finishing a listless and distant third in the Haskell Invitational at Monmouth on August 3. A repeat of that performance would be good for about ninth place.

In addition to Funny Cide, three other three-year-olds were among the ten horses finally entered. These were Dynever, who had finished ahead of Volponi at the Meadowlands; Ten Most Wanted, who'd followed his Travers win with a victory in a $500,000 stakes in Louisiana; and Hold That Tiger, who in his only race in America since shipping over from England had run second to Mineshaft at Belmont.

The six older horses were:

Medaglia d'Oro: trained by Bobby Frankel, ridden by Jerry Bailey, beaten only once in 2003, and by a horse (Candy Ride) that would not run in the Classic.

Perfect Drift: winner of five of seven in 2003, including Grade II stakes in Kentucky and Chicago in September; trained by Australian-born, Kentucky-based Murray Johnson (no relation to P.G.); ridden by *Seabiscuit* actor Gary Stevens.

Pleasantly Perfect: the winner of his first start since March, a Grade II stakes at Santa Anita in early October; trained by low-key and immensely respected California Hall of Famer Richard Mandella, ridden by outstanding California jockey and gentleman Alex Solis.

Congaree: winner of four of seven in 2003, including two at Santa Anita; second to Perfect Drift in his most recent start; trained by non–low-key California Hall of Famer Bob Baffert; ridden by California's leading rider, Patrick Valenzuela.

Evening Attire: third behind Volponi in the Whitney; most recently third in the Jockey Club Gold Cup at Belmont; ridden by most recent Volponi jockey John Velazquez.

Volponi: the biggest horse that P. G. Johnson had ever had, or ever would have.

2 The Johnson family flew out from New York on Wednesday, October 22. I'd made dinner reservations at the Derby, a famed gathering spot for the California racing crowd, adjacent to the Santa Anita track. Unfortunately, I'd neglected to specify a table indoors, and we wound up on a patio hard by the parking lot, where everyone suffered from a temperature that did not drop below 90 until well after the sun had set, and where we swallowed as much smog as water and wine.

But it wouldn't have mattered if we'd been at P.G.'s favorite, the Palm. He was sick with something akin to influenza, and antibioticized into a near stupor. More ominously, just before departure, he'd received the results of another round of medical testing. The presence of a polyp on his vocal cord had been confirmed. Surgery had been scheduled for the following week. Only true grit and a fierce determination neither to be pitied nor to inconvenience anyone carried him through the interminable and mediocre meal. (The Derby: five stars for memorabilia, one for food.)

Frankly, I was made uneasy by his condition. Though

clinging to feistiness, P.G. suddenly seemed a sick and enfee-bled old man. Of course, he *was* sick with an infection, and he had just turned seventy-eight, and he had just endured a flight from New York to Long Beach on JetBlue. He'd also never liked Southern California, and much of the press had begun to make a laughingstock of Volponi—the fluke winner of the 2002 Classic, who had never been able to win another race. These were hardly the ingredients for a festive occasion. If Arlington in 2002 had been a last hurrah, Santa Anita this year seemed more like a noble but doomed last stand.

Eventually, in a voice that faltered more than usual, he managed to tell the story of an earlier California experience, involving Verne Winchell, founder of the Winchell Donut shops that in the 1950s became one of the Los Angeles area's first successful fast-food chains.

"I was out here in '61 and '62, I think. And I had a vet-erinarian called Doc Schmidt. He was Jerkens's vet, Eddie Neloy's vet, Buddy Jacobson's vet: a little guy with a cigarette stuck out of his mouth that he never lit. He was floppy and mopey and two other things: the best vet I ever saw, and as good a friend as anybody will ever have.

"He tells me about how Ron McAnally—whom I did not know at the time, but who I consider it a privilege to know now—was training Donut King, and on the eve of the 1962 Kentucky Derby he was the 8-5 favorite. They have advance betting on the Derby, as you know, and he was 8-5 when the dawn came. Then his hind leg filled up like a balloon and they had to scratch him. Brought him back out here.

"Doc was a married guy with about four kids, but suddenly, because of the horse, he's out here, and the wife and kids are back in New York, and he winds up with a girlfriend. The girlfriend is also Verne Winchell's girlfriend. She was married to a jockey agent named Martin, and her name was Ladine—Ladine Martin. We all called her Ladine the Machine, and she came by that honest.

"Doc kept askin' me, 'Would you like to train this horse? I know what's wrong with him.' He told me some big long name. He says, 'I can straighten this horse out.'

"So the horse comes back out here from Kentucky, and Doc gets a chance to talk to Ladine. He says, 'I'll give him massive doses of Liquamycin.' That's tetracycline, and it had just come on the market. For some reason, that arrested this thing, and the leg went down. Doc tells Ladine, 'I think the leg will be fine, but we can't train him in California because Ron McAnally will find out that I'm injecting him, and I'm not one of his authorized vets.' He winds up explaining it to Ladine in such a way that the only thing for the horse is if Winchell will ship him to me to train in New York.

"Now Winchell is going to approach me. He doesn't know that I already know through Doc, through Ladine the

Machine, that he's gonna ask me to train the horse. So they take me to dinner. I'm sitting in the back seat, and we're driving up someplace, Century Boulevard, I don't know the goddamn streets out here, but it was someplace where you can look down and see the restaurants, see life going on, and we're gonna turn off on an exit and she says, 'Verne, no, don't take Phil there!'

"And he says, 'Why? These steaks are as good as any you can get at the expensive places.' It was Sizzler's, and that's where we went. I never ate one of his donuts, but Verne Winchell was the cheapest human being that ever lived. Ladine said, 'Phil, I'm embarrassed. This cheap son of a bitch!' But he's just smilin' away, and he ate his little steak and I ate mine. And she ate hers, by the way.

"Now, during the meal she brought it up that Doctor Schmidt—Winchell might know about her and Doc Schmidt, but he doesn't care—is a friend of mine, and she says, 'When the meeting is over out here, Phil's going back to New York and Doc Schmidt is going back to New York, and Doc is the only one who can get this medicine for Donut King'—which wasn't true, by the way—'so Ron McAnally won't be able to take care of that leg, so why don't you ship him to Phil in New York?' 'Okay,' Winchell says. No argument. He'd do whatever Ladine told him to do.

"Now that son of a bitch Donut King could really, really,

really, really run. He'd already won the Champagne at Belmont as a two-year-old. Once I got him, we went a mile at Aqueduct in one thirty-four out of the chute, or whatever the record is, you could look that up. Amazing horse.

"Ron McAnally, of course, wasn't happy, but I didn't know him at the time, so it wasn't personal. When I did get to know him, we talked it over, and we're good friends, no problem. In fact, he told me once what a cheap bastard Winchell really was. He'd come to the barn to look at his horses, and they'd go to the backstretch kitchen for coffee and donuts, and not only would Winchell not bring any donuts of his own, he'd make Ron pay for the ones he ate there.

"Anyway, Ron wound up training all the rest of Winchell's horses, and he's been about the best trainer in California since almost before I can remember. Winchell died, I think, last year. He wound up selling his donut shops to Denny's, or one of those blights on the landscape."

Then P.G. said he really wasn't feeling very well, and he asked if someone could drive him back to the hotel in Pasadena.

———

I picked P.G. up at the hotel the next day and took him to Santa Anita. He said he'd slept well, and he seemed slightly more chipper. He was wearing a Volponi baseball cap, but no sunglasses.

"What the hell for?" he said. "I'm not gonna worry about the cataracts until I find out what's going on in my throat."

"How's the horse?"

"Real good. Flying don't bother him nearly as much as it bothers me. Ocala's with him. We'll watch a couple of races, and then go to the barn and take a look. Anyway, I want to introduce him to his new owner."

"New owner?"

"Yeah. Now, for Christ's sake don't say a word about this to anybody, because it's not gonna be announced until next week, but I finally managed to sell him. It was just before I came out here. And it was to Hopewell Farm, a real nice outfit in Midway, Kentucky. The sale takes effect after the race, but how he does in the race can't affect it.

"He'll run for us tomorrow, we'll fly him back to Belmont, and then, toward the end of next week, Ocala will take him down to Kentucky on a van."

In New York, P.G. had told me he'd still been hoping to get at least $3 million for Volponi.

"Did they pay your price?"

"Close. And at least it's done. And to the right sort of place. He'll be in good company. Skip Away is standing at Hopewell."

Even I knew Skip Away: three-year-old of the year in 1996, older male horse of the year in 1997 and 1998, winner of the 1997 Breeders' Cup Classic, winner of scads of other major stakes, second in the Derby and Preakness as a three-year-old, trained by P.G.'s old friend, the late Sonny Hine.

"Better than Japan," I said.

"Better than a lot of places, and as good as any. It takes a lot of pressure off. I don't have to worry about my partner— not that Ed or his group has ever given me any sort of problem—and I know now I'll have something to leave for Kathy and Karen and Emma."

The sale price was only a fraction of the $10 million that members of the Johnson family had permitted themselves to dream about the previous winter, but it assured them that Volponi would leave them with his own head, and theirs, held high, even if there would be tears in some eyes.

I did the arithmetic. "He's earned three million racing, and you sell him for another three, or thereabouts. Not a bad return on twenty-eight thousand dollars."

"What do you mean, he's earned three million racing? The winner's share tomorrow will be another two on top of that."

"Do you really think you'll get it?"

"I think I got as good a shot as anybody. I don't think there's a three-year-old in there good enough to beat the older horses at a mile and a quarter, and the only older one I maybe couldn't beat is Mineshaft, and he's not here. I've run against Medaggily twice, and I beat him six and he beat me one and a half, so how outclassed is that? Congaree's a game horse. I don't know much about Mandella's—what's it called, Perfectly Pleasant?"

"Pleasantly Perfect. Then there's Perfect Drift."

"Well, I don't have to worry about that one, because I'm sure as hell not gonna let myself get beat by another guy named Johnson."

———

As we approached the track, the sky to the east looked gray and oily, even though the sun was blazing and the temperature was approaching 100 degrees.

"Wildfires," I said. "The papers say it happens out here all the time now."

"Why the hell do people live here, will you tell me that? It's a hundred goddamned degrees at the end of October, you can't breathe the air, you got earthquakes, you got fires."

"And floods. Except when there's drought."

"That's all of them, ain't it?"

"All of what?"

"The elements. What the Romans said, or the Greeks. Four elements: fire, air, earth, and water."

"Yeah, and California's oh-for-four. You know, they're selling surgical masks in the drugstores. The television people are saying you should wear them so you don't inhale a bunch of ashes."

"Jesus Christ, that's all I need to do is put on one of those. You get me in that and the sunglasses and the cops will arrest me as a terrorist."

"I don't know. It could make a hell of a winner's circle picture."

"Well, if I get there, you bring down the mask and the glasses and I'll have Ocala put 'em on the horse."

———

There were only about 10,000 people at Santa Anita, but 9,000 of them seemed to be in the clubhouse dining room, where P.G. was supposed to meet the manager of Hopewell Farm.

This proved impossible in the chaos. After an hour, we went to see Volponi in his stall. The people from Hopewell would have ample opportunity to see their new big horse soon enough.

"That ballplayer come around," Ocala said to P.G.

"Who?"

"Pete Rose. He say he wanna see the horse."

"Shit, that's all I need: Volponi wins the race and Pete Rose wins the Pick Six. They'll take me away in handcuffs."

We stood for a while by Volponi's stall. To me, he looked listless, but what did I know? I didn't know this horse. I didn't know any horses. I didn't know how a horse was supposed to look on the eve of a big race after a three-thousand-mile flight into near-100-degree weather, with fires in the hills putting ash into the air. It was probably me who was listless—the horse was fine. At least, I wanted him to be fine. Three months earlier, I couldn't even spell his name. Now, I was starting to get sentimental. P.G., however, was looking at his watch.

"Another goddamned thing about California: Nobody ever thinks they need to be on time."

"Who's coming?"

"The state-licensed vet, who's gonna give this guy a shot of bute."

"You're giving him bute?"

"Can't hurt. He don't need it, but this track is as hard as one of these goddamned freeways, and there's no sense having him distracted by discomfort in the last race of his life."

Phenylbutazone—or Butazolidin—was an anti-inflammatory and pain-relieving drug much favored by horse trainers to alleviate strains and pains caused by training. In New York and a number of other states it was not permitted the day of or the day before a race. California, however, allowed bute if it was administered at least twenty-four hours in advance.

The California vet arrived a few minutes after 4 P.M. and the shot was given with more than an hour to spare. Volponi stood calmly as he received the intravenous injection.

"A professional," the vet said approvingly.

"Always was," P.G. said, and that was as sentimental as he permitted himself to get on the eve of the Classic—at least in public.

3 The fires grew worse overnight. They burned out of control from San Bernardino to San Diego, the most destructive in the recorded history of California.

At Santa Anita, which was shielded from the flames by the San Gabriel Mountains to the east, the temperature shot into the 90s almost as soon as the sun rose. Post time for the first race was 9:40 A.M., to accommodate eastern-oriented television schedules. The Classic would be run at 2:40 Pacific time, as the day's heat neared its peak.

From the moment I arrived at the track, I felt as if my whole recent life in racing—all ninety days of it—was passing before my eyes. Everyone I had met since late July seemed to be in the box-seat area, except Pierre Bellocq, who'd had the good sense to stay home in Princeton and avoid the bedlam.

I tripped over the feet of Barry Schwartz, chairman of the New York Racing Association, and almost fell into the arms of Allen Jerkens's wife before stumbling toward the impeccably dressed Todd Pletcher, and receiving a cordial wave from Bob Baffert, whom I'd never even met, and plopping sweatily into my seat, which turned out to be directly in front of P.G.'s, and just to the left of a grimacing Barclay Tagg.

"It's a very small world, this universe," P.G. had said to me once. "And you got to be careful, because the hand you bite won't feed you."

In Southern California's merciless glare, P.G. looked pale and shrunken and uncomfortable. But Mary Kay and Kathy and Karen and Emma looked terrific, no doubt in new outfits bought especially for the event. "When I die," P.G. had said, "I want my ashes scattered over Bloomingdale's, so I can be close to my family."

The day passed in a rush and a blur. The fires burned, the sun punished, the temperature climbed into the 90s. The Classic was the last of the eight Breeders' Cup races, and for those whose primary interest it was, the tension became as unendurable as the heat.

To my right, Barclay Tagg looked physically healthier than P.G., but almost homicidal or suicidal, I couldn't tell which. I'd always felt—as had P.G.—that Barclay and I might have gotten along if the opportunity had presented itself, but this did not seem the right moment to tell him that. At one point, he nodded a greeting, no doubt having a vague recollection of having seen me somewhere before.

"Your trip out okay?" I said.

"Not really."

The poor bastard. Even if Bobby Frankel didn't feel sorry for him, I did. His trip back would undoubtedly be even worse.

———

There was no shortage of excitement. There was an $83 winner in the Distaff. There was brilliance from Halfbridled (and Julie Krone) in the Juvenile Fillies. There was a shocking last-place finish for Peace Rules in the Mile. There was another Bobby Frankel losing favorite in the Sprint. Irish and English horses swept the first five places in the Filly & Mare Turf. Jerry Bailey finished last on the favorite in the Juvenile, and Edgar Prado finished last in three races in a row. There was a thrilling dead heat in the Turf.

But I was numb to it all. There was only one horse in the world I cared about that afternoon, and as improbable as it was at age sixty, I cared more about him than I'd cared about Chateaugay when I'd been a twenty-year-old at my first Kentucky Derby.

———

As expected, Medaglia d'Oro was the favorite, at 5-2. But he'd been the favorite the year before, I reminded myself, and Volponi had beaten him then. And this year Volponi was only 16-1, not 43-1, and instead of being the longest shot in the field, he was only the second longest, with Evening Attire at 25-1.

The California three-year-old Ten Most Wanted was second choice in the betting at 4-1, followed by Perfect Drift, Congaree, and Hold That Tiger. Funny Cide was 8-1, but if bettors had seen Barclay Tagg's face the way I had all afternoon, he would have been 80-1. Pleasantly Perfect, at 14-1, and Dynever, at 15-1, completed the field.

"The one to watch out for is Pleasantly Perfect," a woman sitting in Barclay Tagg's box said to me.

"How come?"

"If for no other reason, because Dick Mandella has won three of the six races so far."

I had been too preoccupied to notice, but she was right. And two of the wins had come in the two most recent races, with horses that had gone off at 26-1 and 14-1.

As the horses began to file into the starting gate, I shook P.G.'s hand. He nodded, but did not speak. The first and last big horse of his life had raced thirty times over the past four years, but in less than five minutes he'd never race again, and in less than five days he would no longer even be in P.G.'s barn.

One minute, fifty-nine and four-fifths seconds later, it was over.

After dueling with Congaree through most of the race, Medaglia d'Oro finished second for the second consecutive year.

After a very poor start, Dynever charged through the stretch to grab third by a neck.

Congaree hung on for fourth.

Hold That Tiger raced near the front for the first three-quarters of a mile, but wilted in the heat and faded to fifth, a widening five lengths behind Congaree.

Perfect Drift was forced wide on the first turn, made a run at the leaders going into the second turn, but then dropped back to be sixth.

After running last for a mile, Evening Attire wound up seventh.

Ten Most Wanted, who finished eighth, also was pushed very wide in the skirmish on the first turn, and seemed to lose interest in the proceedings.

As Steven Crist had predicted, and as Barclay Tagg's demeanor had foreshadowed, Funny Cide finished ninth.

The *Daily Racing Form* chart said that the winner

was eased back soon after the start, was unhurried along the backstretch, gradually worked his way forward on the far turn, closed the gap between horses to reach contention on the turn, angled four wide nearing the quarter pole, made a run to challenge a sixteenth out then wore down Medaglia d'Oro in the final seventy yards.

It was the description that P.G. had dreamed of for a year. But the horse whose race it described was Pleasantly Perfect.

Of Volponi, the chart said only "failed to mount a serious rally while saving ground."

I would have said, less succinctly, that Volponi was very much in the race for the first six furlongs—in fourth place and only five lengths off the lead—but that about halfway around the final turn he opted for early retirement.

Who knows why? As Jerry Bailey said, they're horses, not machines. The bottom line was that for P.G.'s big horse, thirty-one races turned out to be half a race too many. Santos saw no reason to punish him down the stretch, and let him simply gallop to the wire, five lengths behind Funny Cide.

———

There is absolutely nothing to say—*absolutely* nothing—at the conclusion of the Breeders' Cup Classic when you are sitting between the trainer of the horse who finishes next to last and the trainer of the horse who finishes last. There is not even anywhere to look.

It had been the first time in fourteen races that Volponi had been out of the money, and the first time since the Travers of 2001 that he'd been worse than fourth, and the first time in his life that he'd been last.

The fires raged through the night. P.G.'s flight out the next day was delayed for hours by the smoke.

———

On Tuesday, a surgeon removed a polyp from his vocal cord.

On Thursday, he said good-bye to Volponi, putting the big horse on the van to Kentucky. Tears were shed. Hopewell Farm was the finest of destinations, but something vital to the entire Johnson family had been lost.

Two days later, he suffered another loss. His best remaining horse, She's Got the Beat, sustained a ligament injury during a Grade III stakes race at Aqueduct and had to be retired.

The next week, P.G. learned he had throat cancer. The polyp had been malignant. There was a danger that the cancer might have spread. He would have to undergo three months of intense radiation. The effects would be painful and debilitating, and he received no assurance that the treatment would succeed.

The days now grew very short. Winter moved in. By Thanksgiving, P.G. was so weak and it was so painful for him to try to speak that I could no longer talk to him on the phone. I was east for Christmas, but Mary Kay and Kathy and Karen said he was too sick to see me. Ocala was taking care of the horses. There was no telling when, if ever, P.G. would get back to the barn.

It was not the ending Disney had envisioned.

4 Rockville Centre, 2004

It was not quite spring, but the sun was warm and the temperature was in the upper 60s on March 2, 2004, the day I went back to see P.G. in Rockville Centre.

He had survived. Radiation had rendered him, through the winter, unable even to whisper without pain, or to swallow anything more than baby food. After three months of nausea, weakness, insomnia, and periods of dejection that had dragged him to the brink of despair, he'd been told the day before I saw him that no trace of his cancer remained. His battle had left him stooped and frail, his walk a slow shuffle, his voice still no more than a whisper. But he smiled as he greeted me at 11 A.M.

"I fired two jockeys this morning," he said. "I guess that means I'm gonna live."

He sat in a living room chair, Mary Kay and daughter Kathy nearby. He sipped from a can of ProSure ("a new specialized nutrition and energy beverage formulated specifically to reverse involuntary weight loss associated with cancer, and to help manage involuntary weight loss due to side effects of treatment, including both emotional and physical symptoms").

"I hope you won't be offended if I don't offer you any," he said.

"For heaven's sake, Phil, I can get him a cup of coffee," Mary Kay said.

"How is that stuff?" I asked.

"It ain't Grey Goose, but I need it. They say I lost thirty pounds in three months."

"At least you're here."

"Yeah, and the day before yesterday I even went to the track. First time since before Thanksgiving. Karen took me. One Tough Dude was in the eighth, he ran third, but the reason I went was because my stall list for the spring meet at Belmont was due, and I wanted to deliver it in person: let those bastards know they weren't done with me yet."

"It was also because I wanted him out of the house," Mary Kay said. "He was driving me crazy. You know, he'd been wearing a patch all winter for the pain, and they decided that with the treatment finished it was time to take the patch off. But I think they cut it off too abruptly. I mean, I'm Irish, and I'm of an age where I've seen plenty of drunks, but never before have I had a junkie in my house."

"It was rough for a day or two," P.G. said. "I guess it was, what do they call it, withdrawal."

"We kept a couple of the patches for an emergency, and he kept begging me to put one on him," Mary Kay said. "They're not the kind where you can do it yourself. I said, 'Phil, I'm not going to, because then you'll be back where you started.' He said, 'It's a good thing we don't have a gun in the house, because if I was ever gonna kill someone, it'd be you.' "

"They hadn't warned me how bad it would be," P.G. said. "I guess they never thought I'd get that far."

Mary Kay and Kathy went to the kitchen to prepare lunch.

"*They* thought I was gonna die," P.G. whispered, staring after them. "I guess I did, too. You go from one cancer to another that quick, what's the odds?"

"But you beat it. Again."

"That's what they tell me. I still feel like I'm on death's doormat." He leaned forward in his chair and whispered even more softly: "I welcome each morning, but I fear the night."

He held up a hand. "Maybe 'fear' isn't the right word. But I dread the night."

Mary Kay came back from the kitchen. She said lunch would be sandwiches and pasta salad. "Phil, you should try to have just a little."

"Yeah, yeah, I will." Clearly, this was a dialogue that had wearied them both.

"I still can't swallow real food," P.G. said. "Maybe a little mashed potatoes. Hold on a minute, I want to check." With some difficulty, he raised himself from his chair, and shambled from the living room. He returned a moment later with a flashlight. Then I noticed that there was a bathroom scale in one corner of the room. He stepped onto the scale and shined the light toward the numbers.

"Goddamned cataract, I can't read what the scale says without this light. Let's see . . . one . . . fifty . . . nine . . . point five." He stepped off the scale, switched off the light, and shrugged.

"He does this five times a day," Mary Kay said. "I try to tell him he shouldn't even do it once. It drives him crazy. And you don't gain weight from weighing yourself. Once a week would be enough."

"I got nothin' else to do all day," he rasped. "I can't go to the barn. With the goddamned cataract, I can barely read the paper. I'm not gonna watch the shit that's on television. It's like bein' in a prison. I don't even feel like I'm part of horse racing anymore."

"But, Phil," Mary Kay said, "they're going to remove the cataracts in a couple of weeks. And pretty soon it won't hurt so much to swallow. Once you can start eating, you'll get your strength back."

He put the flashlight away and returned to his chair. "It's hard for me to believe," he said, "but the surgeon told me yesterday that by August I oughta be a hundred percent."

"Just in time for Saratoga," I said.

"Saratoga. I gotta tell you something: There's some researcher up there has been digging into it, and he's just informed me that I haven't won a race there however many years in a row. He says I missed one way back when."

"Is he right?"

"He might be. When I started thinkin' about it, there was one year I don't think I went, because my horses weren't good enough. That was the year they experimented with a summer meet at Laurel, in Maryland, and I went down there instead. So I guess I get back to Saratoga this summer and they'll expose me as a fraud."

"Probably drum you out of the Hall of Fame," I said.

"If they do, I'll give my place to Barclay. He deserves it just for surviving."

Barclay Tagg had spent the winter in Florida. He'd run Funny Cide twice since January 1, when the horse had turned four. Funny Cide had run well and had come close, but lost— first to Medaglia d'Oro at Gulfstream, then to Peace Rules in New Orleans. He was threatening to become the Volponi of 2004. This did not seem a comment I needed to make to P.G.

"Have you heard from Barclay?" I asked instead.

"Let me tell you something: Barclay has been calling me every couple of days through it all. No one—no one—could have been a better friend to Mary Kay and me through the worst of this than Barclay has been. There's been others: John

Hertler, who was my assistant before Ocala, Jean-Luc Samyn, who's been riding for me for years, but they're family. And Mike Lakow, the racing secretary here, he's been great. But I gotta tell you, there's been nobody has shown he's cared more than Barclay."

"How about Jerkens?"

"I haven't heard a word from Allen. He's never called. Not once."

There was a pause. Mary Kay started to say something, but stopped herself. P.G. shrugged and looked down at the floor again. It seemed like a good subject to change.

"How's the big horse enjoying Kentucky?"

He looked up and grinned. "More than he enjoyed California. You know, I scoped him after he got back, and his trachea was full of blood and mucus. That's why he didn't keep running: On that far turn, he must've been starting to choke."

"What would have caused that?"

"Probably all that shit you had in the air out there. It can't do a horse good to breathe ashes in when he's tryin' to run his heart out. And the heat can't have helped. All I know is he'd never been like that before, not once, anywhere. I think out there is a tough environment to get used to, at least for a horse. Nobody from New York did any good. I'll tell you something else: I knew we were dead when I saw him in the paddock before the race. He looked okay, but when I touched him he was cold and clammy. Cold and clammy! In that weather."

"Why?"

"Coulda been anything. It could even have been the bute I gave him the day before. I don't know. You spend your whole life with racehorses and there's still so much you'll never know. But he's makin' 'em sit up and take notice in Kentucky. The breeding season started on February 15. A couple of days ago they called me from Hopewell and said, 'This horse is amazing: he's a *breeding machine!*' "

P.G. smiled proudly, as if he'd trained Volponi to be a stud, too.

"A couple more years and you'll see the results," I said.

"I hope I don't have to wait that long for something good. I might not be here."

"How do the new two-year-olds look?"

He smiled again and nodded slowly. "All I know so far is what they tell me from Florida and what I see on the videos they send me, but a couple of 'em might be worth their feed bill. I got a Swain filly out of a mare called As Long As It Takes. I named her Wait It Out. Story of my life: As long as it takes, wait it out."

"Tell him about the colt, Phil," Mary Kay said.

"Yeeaah," he said, drawing out the sound. "I got a Chester House colt I named Port Chester. I bought him as a weanling in November of 2002 for almost a hundred and fifty thousand, which is the most of my own money I ever paid for a horse. I guess I was still nuts after winning the Classic. He looks like a big, tough son of a bitch—like Volponi. He's not gonna set any records in two-year-old sprints, but by his pedigree he could get to be something special."

"Another big horse?"

"You never know," he said, smiling. "We might get lucky."

He said his new two-year-olds would be arriving from Florida on April 1.

"And you'll be at the barn to greet them?"

"With open arms," he said, giving his biggest smile of the day. "What do you think kept me alive all winter long?"

Volponi in retirement

Epilogue

P.G.'s recovery did not progress as he had hoped, and he was not well enough to be back at his barn by April 1.

But from his home in Rockville Centre, as he continued to battle to regain his strength, P.G. accomplished one of the most remarkable training feats of his entire career.

The cataract surgery in early March had been successful, and P.G. again was able to read the "condition book"—the published list compiled by a track's racing secretary that describes the types of races to be run each day. It is by a close perusal of the condition book that a skilled trainer can determine which sort of upcoming race might be most suitable for a particular horse.

Able to see clearly again, P.G. pored over the condition book for the Aqueduct spring meeting—set to begin on March 10—the way a religious man in similar straits might have attended to Scripture.

He also determined what type of workout he wanted each horse to have each morning, transmitting those instructions, in writing, to Ocala.

On the day of a race, he whispered riding instructions to Mary Kay, who communicated them by telephone to the jockey or jockey's agent.

And in this manner, like a grandmaster at a chess table, P.G. orchestrated a four-week streak that ranked among his most extraordinary.

Eleven of his thirteen starters finished in the money at Aqueduct between March 10 and April 6. Five of them won. Through the first four weeks of the meeting, P.G. led all New York trainers (including the 2003 Saratoga leader, Todd Pletcher) both in winning percentage (38) and in-the-money percentage (85). And he'd done it without being able to go either to the racetrack or to the barn.

"This is very gratifying to all of us," P.G.'s daughter Kathy wrote to me by e-mail in early April, "because whatever strength my dad has at the moment has been directed at training and placing these horses."

It seemed that there was life after the big horse, after all.